On
Managing Yourself

HBR'S 10 MUST READS

On Managing Yourself

HARVARD BUSINESS REVIEW PRESS
Boston, Massachusetts

The web addresses referenced in this book were live and correct at the time of
the book's publication but may be subject to change.

Library of Congress Cataloging-in-Publication Data

HBR's 10 must reads on managing yourself.
    p. cm.
  Includes index.
  ISBN 978-1-4221-5799-2 (pbk. : alk paper)
  1. Management. I. Harvard business review. II. Title: HBR's ten must
reads on managing yourself. III. Title: Harvard business review's 10 must
reads on managing yourself.
  HD31.H3946 2010

ISBN: 9781422157992
eISBN: 9781422172032

Contents

HBR'S
10
MUST
READS

On
Managing Yourself

How Will You Measure Your Life?

by Clayton M. Christensen

BEFORE I PUBLISHED *The Innovator's Dilemma,* I got a call from Andrew Grove, then the chairman of Intel. He had read one of my early papers about disruptive technology, and he asked if I could talk to his direct reports and explain my research and what it implied for Intel. Excited, I flew to Silicon Valley and showed up at the appointed time, only to have Grove say, "Look, stuff has happened. We have only 10 minutes for you. Tell us what your model of disruption means for Intel." I said that I couldn't—that I needed a full 30 minutes to explain the model, because only with it as context would any comments about Intel make sense. Ten minutes into my explanation, Grove interrupted: "Look, I've got your model. Just tell us what it means for Intel."

I insisted that I needed 10 more minutes to describe how the process of disruption had worked its way through a very different industry, steel, so that he and his team could understand how disruption worked. I told the story of how Nucor and other steel minimills had begun by attacking the lowest end of the market—steel reinforcing bars, or rebar—and later moved up toward the high end, undercutting the traditional steel mills.

When I finished the minimill story, Grove said, "OK, I get it. What it means for Intel is …," and then went on to articulate what would become the company's strategy for going to the bottom of the market to launch the Celeron processor.

I've thought about that a million times since. If I had been suckered into telling Andy Grove what he should think about the microprocessor business, I'd have been killed. But instead of telling him what to think, I taught him how to think—and then he reached what I felt was the correct decision on his own.

That experience had a profound influence on me. When people ask what I think they should do, I rarely answer their question directly. Instead, I run the question aloud through one of my models. I'll describe how the process in the model worked its way through an industry quite different from their own. And then, more often than not, they'll say, "OK, I get it." And they'll answer their own question more insightfully than I could have.

My class at HBS is structured to help my students understand what good management theory is and how it is built. To that backbone I attach different models or theories that help students think about the various dimensions of a general manager's job in stimulating innovation and growth. In each session we look at one company through the lenses of those theories—using them to explain how the company got into its situation and to examine what managerial actions will yield the needed results.

On the last day of class, I ask my students to turn those theoretical lenses on themselves, to find cogent answers to three questions: First, how can I be sure that I'll be happy in my career? Second, how can I be sure that my relationships with my spouse and my family become an enduring source of happiness? Third, how can I be sure I'll stay out of jail? Though the last question sounds lighthearted, it's not. Two of the 32 people in my Rhodes scholar class spent time in jail. Jeff Skilling of Enron fame was a classmate of mine at HBS. These were good guys—but something in their lives sent them off in the wrong direction.

Idea in Brief

Harvard Business School's Christensen teaches aspiring MBAs how to apply management and innovation theories to build stronger companies. But he also believes that these models can help people lead better lives. In this article, he explains how, exploring questions everyone needs to ask. How can I be happy in my career? How can I be sure that my relationship with my family is an enduring source of happiness? And how can I live my life with integrity? The answer to the first question comes from Frederick Herzberg's assertion that the most powerful motivator isn't money; it's the opportunity to learn, grow in responsibilities, contribute, and be recognized. That's why management, if practiced well, can be the noblest of occupations; no others offer as many ways to help people find those opportunities. It isn't about buying, selling, and investing in companies, as many think. The principles of resource allocation can help people attain happiness at home. If not managed masterfully, what emerges from a firm's resource allocation process can be very different from the strategy management intended to follow. That's true in life too: If you're not guided by a clear sense of purpose, you're likely to fritter away your time and energy on obtaining the most tangible, short-term signs of achievement, not what's really important to you. And just as a focus on marginal costs can cause bad corporate decisions, it can lead people astray. The marginal cost of doing something wrong "just this once" always seems alluringly low. You don't see the end result to which that path leads. The key is to define what you stand for and draw the line in a safe place.

As the students discuss the answers to these questions, I open my own life to them as a case study of sorts, to illustrate how they can use the theories from our course to guide their life decisions.

One of the theories that gives great insight on the first question—how to be sure we find happiness in our careers—is from Frederick Herzberg, who asserts that the powerful motivator in our lives isn't money; it's the opportunity to learn, grow in responsibilities, contribute to others, and be recognized for achievements. I tell the students about a vision of sorts I had while I was running the company I founded before becoming an academic. In my mind's eye I saw one of my managers leave for work one morning with a relatively strong level of self-esteem. Then I pictured her driving home to her family 10 hours later, feeling unappreciated, frustrated, underutilized, and demeaned. I imagined how profoundly her lowered self-esteem affected the way she interacted with her children. The vision in my mind then fast-forwarded to another day, when she drove home with greater self-esteem—feeling that she had learned a lot, been recognized for achieving valuable things, and played a significant role in the success of some important initiatives. I then imagined how positively that affected her as a spouse and a parent. My conclusion: Management is the most noble of professions if it's practiced well. No other occupation offers as many ways to help others learn and grow, take responsibility and be recognized for achievement, and contribute to the success of a team. More and more MBA students come to school thinking that a career in business means buying, selling, and investing in companies. That's unfortunate. Doing deals doesn't yield the deep rewards that come from building up people.

I want students to leave my classroom knowing that.

Create a Strategy for Your Life

A theory that is helpful in answering the second question—How can I ensure that my relationship with my family proves to be an enduring source of happiness?—concerns how strategy is defined and implemented. Its primary insight is that a company's strategy is determined by the types of initiatives that management invests in. If a company's resource allocation process is not managed masterfully, what emerges from it can be very different from what management intended. Because companies' decision-making systems are designed to steer investments to initiatives that offer the most tangible and immediate returns, companies shortchange investments in initiatives that are crucial to their long-term strategies.

Over the years I've watched the fates of my HBS classmates from 1979 unfold; I've seen more and more of them come to reunions unhappy, divorced, and alienated from their children. I can guarantee you that not a single one of them graduated with the deliberate strategy of getting divorced and raising children who would become estranged from them. And yet a shocking number of them implemented that strategy. The reason? They didn't keep the purpose of their lives front and center as they decided how to spend their time, talents, and energy.

It's quite startling that a significant fraction of the 900 students that HBS draws each year from the world's best have given little thought to the purpose of their lives. I tell the students that HBS might be one of their last chances to reflect deeply on that question. If they think that they'll have more time and energy to reflect later, they're nuts, because life only gets more demanding: You take on a mortgage; you're working 70 hours a week; you have a spouse and children.

For me, having a clear purpose in my life has been essential. But it was something I had to think long and hard about before I understood it. When I was a Rhodes scholar, I was in a very demanding academic program, trying to cram an extra year's worth of work into my time at Oxford. I decided to spend an hour every night reading, thinking, and praying about why God put me on this earth. That was a very challenging commitment to keep, because every hour I spent doing that, I wasn't studying applied econometrics. I was conflicted about whether I could really afford to take that time away from my studies, but I stuck with it—and ultimately figured out the purpose of my life.

Had I instead spent that hour each day learning the latest techniques for mastering the problems of autocorrelation in regression analysis, I would have badly misspent my life. I apply the tools of econometrics a few times a year, but I apply my knowledge of the purpose of my life every day. It's the single most useful thing I've ever learned. I promise my students that if they take the time to figure out their life purpose, they'll look back on it as the most important thing they discovered at HBS. If they don't figure it out, they will just sail off without a rudder and get buffeted in the very rough seas of life. Clarity about their purpose will trump knowledge of activity-based costing, balanced scorecards, core competence, disruptive innovation, the four Ps, and the five forces.

My purpose grew out of my religious faith, but faith isn't the only thing that gives people direction. For example, one of my former

The Class of 2010

"**I CAME TO BUSINESS SCHOOL** knowing exactly what I wanted to do—and I'm leaving choosing the exact opposite. I've worked in the private sector all my life, because everyone always told me that's where smart people are. But I've decided to try government and see if I can find more meaning there.

"I used to think that industry was very safe. The recession has shown us that nothing is safe."

Ruhana Hafiz, Harvard Business School, Class of 2010
Her Plans: To join the FBI as a special adviser (a management track position)

"You could see a shift happening at HBS. Money used to be number one in the job search. When you make a ton of money, you want more of it. Ironic thing. You start to forget what the drivers of happiness are and what things are really important. A lot of people on campus see money differently now. They think, 'What's the minimum I need to have, and what else drives my life?' instead of 'What's the place where I can get the maximum of both?'"

Patrick Chun, Harvard Business School, Class of 2010
His Plans: To join Bain Capital

"The financial crisis helped me realize that you have to do what you really love in life. My current vision of success is based on the impact I can have, the

students decided that his purpose was to bring honesty and economic prosperity to his country and to raise children who were as capably committed to this cause, and to each other, as he was. His purpose is focused on family and others—as mine is.

The choice and successful pursuit of a profession is but one tool for achieving your purpose. But without a purpose, life can become hollow.

Allocate Your Resources

Your decisions about allocating your personal time, energy, and talent ultimately shape your life's strategy.

I have a bunch of "businesses" that compete for these resources: I'm trying to have a rewarding relationship with my wife, raise great kids, contribute to my community, succeed in my career, contribute experiences I can gain, and the happiness I can find personally, much more so than the pursuit of money or prestige. My main motivations are (1) to be with my family and people I care about; (2) to do something fun, exciting, and impactful; and (3) to pursue a long-term career in entrepreneurship, where I can build companies that change the way the world works."

Matt Salzberg, Harvard Business School, Class of 2010
His Plans: To work for Bessemer Venture Partners

"Because I'm returning to McKinsey, it probably seems like not all that much has changed for me. But while I was at HBS, I decided to do the dual degree at the Kennedy School. With the elections in 2008 and the economy looking shaky, it seemed more compelling for me to get a better understanding of the public and nonprofit sectors. In a way, that drove my return to McKinsey, where I'll have the ability to explore private, public, and nonprofit sectors.

"The recession has made us step back and take stock of how lucky we are. The crisis to us is 'Are we going to have a job by April?' Crisis to a lot of people is 'Are we going to stay in our home?'"

John Coleman, Harvard Business School, Class of 2010
His Plans: To return to McKinsey & Company

to my church, and so on. And I have exactly the same problem that a corporation does. I have a limited amount of time and energy and talent. How much do I devote to each of these pursuits?

Allocation choices can make your life turn out to be very different from what you intended. Sometimes that's good: Opportunities that you never planned for emerge. But if you misinvest your resources, the outcome can be bad. As I think about my former classmates who inadvertently invested for lives of hollow unhappiness, I can't help believing that their troubles relate right back to a short-term perspective.

When people who have a high need for achievement—and that includes all Harvard Business School graduates—have an extra half hour of time or an extra ounce of energy, they'll unconsciously allocate it to activities that yield the most tangible accomplishments. And our careers provide the most concrete evidence that we're moving forward. You ship a product, finish a design, complete a presentation, close a sale, teach a class, publish a paper, get paid, get promoted. In contrast, investing time and energy in your relationship with your spouse and children typically doesn't offer that same immediate sense of achievement. Kids misbehave every day. It's really not until 20 years down the road that you can put your hands on your hips and say, "I raised a good son or a good daughter." You can neglect your relationship with your spouse, and on a day-to-day basis, it doesn't seem as if things are deteriorating. People who are driven to excel have this unconscious propensity to underinvest in their families and overinvest in their careers—even though intimate and loving relationships with their families are the most powerful and enduring source of happiness.

If you study the root causes of business disasters, over and over you'll find this predisposition toward endeavors that offer immediate gratification. If you look at personal lives through that lens, you'll see the same stunning and sobering pattern: people allocating fewer and fewer resources to the things they would have once said mattered most.

Create a Culture

There's an important model in our class called the Tools of Cooperation, which basically says that being a visionary manager isn't all it's cracked up to be. It's one thing to see into the foggy future with acuity and chart the course corrections that the company must make. But it's quite another to persuade employees who might not see the changes ahead to line up and work cooperatively to take the company in that new direction. Knowing what tools to wield to elicit the needed cooperation is a critical managerial skill.

The theory arrays these tools along two dimensions—the extent to which members of the organization agree on what they want from their participation in the enterprise, and the extent to which they agree on what actions will produce the desired results. When there is little agreement on both axes, you have to use "power tools"—coercion, threats, punishment, and so on—to secure cooperation.

Many companies start in this quadrant, which is why the founding executive team must play such an assertive role in defining what must be done and how. If employees' ways of working together to address those tasks succeed over and over, consensus begins to form. MIT's Edgar Schein has described this process as the mechanism by which a culture is built. Ultimately, people don't even think about whether their way of doing things yields success. They embrace priorities and follow procedures by instinct and assumption rather than by explicit decision—which means that they've created a culture. Culture, in compelling but unspoken ways, dictates the proven, acceptable methods by which members of the group address recurrent problems. And culture defines the priority given to different types of problems. It can be a powerful management tool.

In using this model to address the question, How can I be sure that my family becomes an enduring source of happiness?, my students quickly see that the simplest tools that parents can wield to elicit cooperation from children are power tools. But there comes a point during the teen years when power tools no longer work. At that point parents start wishing that they had begun working with their children at a very young age to build a culture at home in which children instinctively behave respectfully toward one another, obey their parents, and choose the right thing to do. Families have cultures, just as companies do. Those cultures can be built consciously or evolve inadvertently.

If you want your kids to have strong self-esteem and confidence that they can solve hard problems, those qualities won't magically materialize in high school. You have to design them into your family's culture—and you have to think about this very early on. Like employees, children build self-esteem by doing things that are hard and learning what works.

Avoid the "Marginal Costs" Mistake

We're taught in finance and economics that in evaluating alternative investments, we should ignore sunk and fixed costs, and instead base decisions on the marginal costs and marginal revenues that each alternative entails. We learn in our course that this doctrine biases companies to leverage what they have put in place to succeed in the past, instead of guiding them to create the capabilities they'll need in the future. If we knew the future would be exactly the same as the past, that approach would be fine. But if the future's different—and it almost always is—then it's the wrong thing to do.

This theory addresses the third question I discuss with my students—how to live a life of integrity (stay out of jail). Unconsciously, we often employ the marginal cost doctrine in our personal lives when we choose between right and wrong. A voice in our head says, "Look, I know that as a general rule, most people shouldn't do this. But in this particular extenuating circumstance, just this once, it's OK." The marginal cost of doing something wrong "just this once" always seems alluringly low. It suckers you in, and you don't ever look at where that path ultimately is headed and at the full costs that the choice entails. Justification for infidelity and dishonesty in all their manifestations lies in the marginal cost economics of "just this once."

I'd like to share a story about how I came to understand the potential damage of "just this once" in my own life. I played on the Oxford University varsity basketball team. We worked our tails off and finished the season undefeated. The guys on the team were the best friends I've ever had in my life. We got to the British equivalent of the NCAA tournament—and made it to the final four. It turned out the championship game was scheduled to be played on a Sunday. I had made a personal commitment to God at age 16 that I would never play ball on Sunday. So I went to the coach and explained my problem. He was incredulous. My teammates were, too, because I was the starting center. Every one of the guys on the team came to me and said, "You've got to play. Can't you break the rule just this one time?"

I'm a deeply religious man, so I went away and prayed about what I should do. I got a very clear feeling that I shouldn't break my commitment—so I didn't play in the championship game.

In many ways that was a small decision—involving one of several thousand Sundays in my life. In theory, surely I could have crossed over the line just that one time and then not done it again. But looking back on it, resisting the temptation whose logic was "In this extenuating circumstance, just this once, it's OK" has proven to be one of the most important decisions of my life. Why? My life has been one unending stream of extenuating circumstances. Had I crossed the line that one time, I would have done it over and over in the years that followed.

The lesson I learned from this is that it's easier to hold to your principles 100% of the time than it is to hold to them 98% of the time. If you give in to "just this once," based on a marginal cost analysis, as some of my former classmates have done, you'll regret where you end up. You've got to define for yourself what you stand for and draw the line in a safe place.

Remember the Importance of Humility

I got this insight when I was asked to teach a class on humility at Harvard College. I asked all the students to describe the most humble person they knew. One characteristic of these humble people stood out: They had a high level of self-esteem. They knew who they were, and they felt good about who they were. We also decided that humility was defined not by self-deprecating behavior or attitudes but by the esteem with which you regard others. Good behavior flows naturally from that kind of humility. For example, you would never steal from someone, because you respect that person too much. You'd never lie to someone, either.

It's crucial to take a sense of humility into the world. By the time you make it to a top graduate school, almost all your learning has come from people who are smarter and more experienced than you: parents, teachers, bosses. But once you've finished at Harvard Business School or any other top academic institution, the vast majority of people you'll interact with on a day-to-day basis may not be smarter than you. And if your attitude is that only smarter people have something to teach you, your learning opportunities will be very limited. But if you have a humble eagerness to learn something from everybody, your learning opportunities will be unlimited.

Generally, you can be humble only if you feel really good about yourself—and you want to help those around you feel really good about themselves, too. When we see people acting in an abusive, arrogant, or demeaning manner toward others, their behavior almost always is a symptom of their lack of self-esteem. They need to put someone else down to feel good about themselves.

Choose the Right Yardstick

This past year I was diagnosed with cancer and faced the possibility that my life would end sooner than I'd planned. Thankfully, it now looks as if I'll be spared. But the experience has given me important insight into my life.

I have a pretty clear idea of how my ideas have generated enormous revenue for companies that have used my research; I know I've had a substantial impact. But as I've confronted this disease, it's been interesting to see how unimportant that impact is to me now. I've concluded that the metric by which God will assess my life isn't dollars but the individual people whose lives I've touched.

I think that's the way it will work for us all. Don't worry about the level of individual prominence you have achieved; worry about the individuals you have helped become better people. This is my final recommendation: Think about the metric by which your life will be judged, and make a resolution to live every day so that in the end, your life will be judged a success.

Originally published in July 2010. Reprint R1007B

Managing Oneself

by Peter F. Drucker

HISTORY'S GREAT ACHIEVERS—a Napoléon, a da Vinci, a Mozart—have always managed themselves. That, in large measure, is what makes them great achievers. But they are rare exceptions, so unusual both in their talents and their accomplishments as to be considered outside the boundaries of ordinary human existence. Now, most of us, even those of us with modest endowments, will have to learn to manage ourselves. We will have to learn to develop ourselves. We will have to place ourselves where we can make the greatest contribution. And we will have to stay mentally alert and engaged during a 50-year working life, which means knowing how and when to change the work we do.

What Are My Strengths?

Most people think they know what they are good at. They are usually wrong. More often, people know what they are not good at—and even then more people are wrong than right. And yet, a person can perform only from strength. One cannot build performance on weaknesses, let alone on something one cannot do at all.

Throughout history, people had little need to know their strengths. A person was born into a position and a line of work: The peasant's son would also be a peasant; the artisan's daughter, an artisan's wife; and so on. But now people have choices. We need to know our strengths in order to know where we belong.

The only way to discover your strengths is through feedback analysis. Whenever you make a key decision or take a key action, write down what you expect will happen. Nine or 12 months later, compare the actual results with your expectations. I have been practicing this method for 15 to 20 years now, and every time I do it, I am surprised. The feedback analysis showed me, for instance—and to my great surprise—that I have an intuitive understanding of technical people, whether they are engineers or accountants or market researchers. It also showed me that I don't really resonate with generalists.

Feedback analysis is by no means new. It was invented sometime in the fourteenth century by an otherwise totally obscure German theologian and picked up quite independently, some 150 years later, by John Calvin and Ignatius of Loyola, each of whom incorporated it into the practice of his followers. In fact, the steadfast focus on performance and results that this habit produces explains why the institutions these two men founded, the Calvinist church and the Jesuit order, came to dominate Europe within 30 years.

Practiced consistently, this simple method will show you within a fairly short period of time, maybe two or three years, where your strengths lie—and this is the most important thing to know. The method will show you what you are doing or failing to do that deprives you of the full benefits of your strengths. It will show you where you are not particularly competent. And finally, it will show you where you have no strengths and cannot perform.

Several implications for action follow from feedback analysis. First and foremost, concentrate on your strengths. Put yourself where your strengths can produce results.

Second, work on improving your strengths. Analysis will rapidly show where you need to improve skills or acquire new ones. It will also show the gaps in your knowledge—and those can usually be filled. Mathematicians are born, but everyone can learn trigonometry.

Third, discover where your intellectual arrogance is causing disabling ignorance and overcome it. Far too many people—especially

Idea in Brief

We live in an age of unprecedented opportunity: If you've got ambition, drive, and smarts, you can rise to the top of your chosen profession—regardless of where you started out. But with opportunity comes responsibility. Companies today aren't managing their knowledge workers' careers. Rather, we must each be our own chief executive officer.

Simply put, it's up to you to carve out your place in the work world and know when to change course. And it's up to you to keep yourself engaged and productive during a work life that may span some 50 years.

To do all of these things well, you'll need to cultivate a deep understanding of yourself. What are your most valuable strengths and most dangerous weaknesses? Equally important, how do you learn and work with others? What are your most deeply held values? And in what type of work environment can you make the greatest contribution?

The implication is clear: Only when you operate from a combination of your strengths and self-knowledge can you achieve true—and lasting— excellence.

people with great expertise in one area—are contemptuous of knowledge in other areas or believe that being bright is a substitute for knowledge. First-rate engineers, for instance, tend to take pride in not knowing anything about people. Human beings, they believe, are much too disorderly for the good engineering mind. Human resources professionals, by contrast, often pride themselves on their ignorance of elementary accounting or of quantitative methods altogether. But taking pride in such ignorance is self-defeating. Go to work on acquiring the skills and knowledge you need to fully realize your strengths.

It is equally essential to remedy your bad habits—the things you do or fail to do that inhibit your effectiveness and performance. Such habits will quickly show up in the feedback. For example, a planner may find that his beautiful plans fail because he does not follow through on them. Like so many brilliant people, he believes that ideas move mountains. But bulldozers move mountains; ideas show where the bulldozers should go to work. This planner will have to learn that the work does not stop when the plan is completed. He

Idea in Practice

To build a life of excellence, begin by asking yourself these questions:

"What are my strengths?"

To accurately identify your strengths, use **feedback analysis**. Every time you make a key decision, write down the outcome you expect. Several months later, compare the actual results with your expected results. Look for patterns in what you're seeing: What results are you skilled at generating? What abilities do you need to enhance in order to get the results you want? What unproductive habits are preventing you from creating the outcomes you desire? In identifying opportunities for improvement, don't waste time cultivating skill areas where you have little competence. Instead, concentrate on—and build on—your strengths.

"How do I work?"

In what ways do you work best? Do you process information most effectively by reading it, or by hearing others discuss it? Do you accomplish the most by working with other people, or by working alone? Do you perform best while making decisions, or while advising others on key matters? Are you in top form when things get stressful, or do you function optimally in a highly predictable environment?

"What are my values?"

What are your ethics? What do you see as your most important responsibilities for living a worthy, ethical life? Do your organization's ethics resonate with your own values? If not, your career will likely be marked by frustration and poor performance.

"Where do I belong?"

Consider your strengths, preferred work style, and values. Based on these qualities, in what kind of work environment would you fit in best? Find the perfect fit, and you'll transform yourself from a merely acceptable employee into a star performer.

"What can I contribute?"

In earlier eras, companies told businesspeople what their contribution should be. Today, you have choices. To decide how you can best enhance your organization's performance, first ask what the situation requires. Based on your strengths, work style, and values, how might you make the greatest contribution to your organization's efforts?

must find people to carry out the plan and explain it to them. He must adapt and change it as he puts it into action. And finally, he must decide when to stop pushing the plan.

At the same time, feedback will also reveal when the problem is a lack of manners. Manners are the lubricating oil of an organization. It is a law of nature that two moving bodies in contact with each other create friction. This is as true for human beings as it is for inanimate objects. Manners—simple things like saying "please" and "thank you" and knowing a person's name or asking after her family—enable two people to work together whether they like each other or not. Bright people, especially bright young people, often do not understand this. If analysis shows that someone's brilliant work fails again and again as soon as cooperation from others is required, it probably indicates a lack of courtesy—that is, a lack of manners.

Comparing your expectations with your results also indicates what not to do. We all have a vast number of areas in which we have no talent or skill and little chance of becoming even mediocre. In those areas a person—and especially a knowledge worker—should not take on work, jobs, and assignments. One should waste as little effort as possible on improving areas of low competence. It takes far more energy and work to improve from incompetence to mediocrity than it takes to improve from first-rate performance to excellence. And yet most people—especially most teachers and most organizations—concentrate on making incompetent performers into mediocre ones. Energy, resources, and time should go instead to making a competent person into a star performer.

How Do I Perform?

Amazingly few people know how they get things done. Indeed, most of us do not even know that different people work and perform differently. Too many people work in ways that are not their ways, and that almost guarantees nonperformance. For knowledge workers, How do I perform? may be an even more important question than What are my strengths?

Like one's strengths, how one performs is unique. It is a matter of personality. Whether personality be a matter of nature or nurture, it surely is formed long before a person goes to work. And *how* a person performs is a given, just as *what* a person is good at or not good at is a given. A person's way of performing can be slightly modified, but it is unlikely to be completely changed—and certainly not easily. Just as people achieve results by doing what they are good at, they also achieve results by working in ways that they best perform. A few common personality traits usually determine how a person performs.

Am I a reader or a listener?

The first thing to know is whether you are a reader or a listener. Far too few people even know that there are readers and listeners and that people are rarely both. Even fewer know which of the two they themselves are. But some examples will show how damaging such ignorance can be.

When Dwight Eisenhower was Supreme Commander of the Allied forces in Europe, he was the darling of the press. His press conferences were famous for their style—General Eisenhower showed total command of whatever question he was asked, and he was able to describe a situation and explain a policy in two or three beautifully polished and elegant sentences. Ten years later, the same journalists who had been his admirers held President Eisenhower in open contempt. He never addressed the questions, they complained, but rambled on endlessly about something else. And they constantly ridiculed him for butchering the King's English in incoherent and ungrammatical answers.

Eisenhower apparently did not know that he was a reader, not a listener. When he was Supreme Commander in Europe, his aides made sure that every question from the press was presented in writing at least half an hour before a conference was to begin. And then Eisenhower was in total command. When he became president, he succeeded two listeners, Franklin D. Roosevelt and Harry Truman. Both men knew themselves to be listeners and both enjoyed free-for-all press conferences. Eisenhower may have felt that he had to do what his two predecessors had done. As a result, he never even heard the questions journalists asked. And Eisenhower is not even an extreme case of a nonlistener.

A few years later, Lyndon Johnson destroyed his presidency, in large measure, by not knowing that he was a listener. His predecessor, John Kennedy, was a reader who had assembled a brilliant group of writers as his assistants, making sure that they wrote to him before discussing their memos in person. Johnson kept these people on his staff—and they kept on writing. He never, apparently, understood one word of what they wrote. Yet as a senator, Johnson had been superb; for parliamentarians have to be, above all, listeners.

Few listeners can be made, or can make themselves, into competent readers—and vice versa. The listener who tries to be a reader will, therefore, suffer the fate of Lyndon Johnson, whereas the reader who tries to be a listener will suffer the fate of Dwight Eisenhower. They will not perform or achieve.

How do I learn?

The second thing to know about how one performs is to know how one learns. Many first-class writers—Winston Churchill is but one example—do poorly in school. They tend to remember their schooling as pure torture. Yet few of their classmates remember it the same way. They may not have enjoyed the school very much, but the worst they suffered was boredom. The explanation is that writers do not, as a rule, learn by listening and reading. They learn by writing. Because schools do not allow them to learn this way, they get poor grades.

Schools everywhere are organized on the assumption that there is only one right way to learn and that it is the same way for everybody. But to be forced to learn the way a school teaches is sheer hell for students who learn differently. Indeed, there are probably half a dozen different ways to learn.

There are people, like Churchill, who learn by writing. Some people learn by taking copious notes. Beethoven, for example, left behind an enormous number of sketchbooks, yet he said he never actually looked at them when he composed. Asked why he kept them, he is reported to have replied, "If I don't write it down immediately, I forget it right away. If I put it into a sketchbook, I never forget it and I never have to look it up again." Some people learn by doing. Others learn by hearing themselves talk.

A chief executive I know who converted a small and mediocre family business into the leading company in its industry was one of those people who learn by talking. He was in the habit of calling his entire senior staff into his office once a week and then talking at them for two or three hours. He would raise policy issues and argue three different positions on each one. He rarely asked his associates for comments or questions; he simply needed an audience to hear himself talk. That's how he learned. And although he is a fairly extreme case, learning through talking is by no means an unusual method. Successful trial lawyers learn the same way, as do many medical diagnosticians (and so do I).

Of all the important pieces of self-knowledge, understanding how you learn is the easiest to acquire. When I ask people, "How do you learn?" most of them know the answer. But when I ask, "Do you act on this knowledge?" few answer yes. And yet, acting on this knowledge is the key to performance; or rather, *not* acting on this knowledge condemns one to nonperformance.

Am I a reader or a listener? and How do I learn? are the first questions to ask. But they are by no means the only ones. To manage yourself effectively, you also have to ask, Do I work well with people, or am I a loner? And if you do work well with people, you then must ask, In what relationship?

Some people work best as subordinates. General George Patton, the great American military hero of World War II, is a prime example. Patton was America's top troop commander. Yet when he was proposed for an independent command, General George Marshall, the U.S. chief of staff—and probably the most successful picker of men in U.S. history—said, "Patton is the best subordinate the American army has ever produced, but he would be the worst commander."

Some people work best as team members. Others work best alone. Some are exceptionally talented as coaches and mentors; others are simply incompetent as mentors.

Another crucial question is, Do I produce results as a decision maker or as an adviser? A great many people perform best as advisers but cannot take the burden and pressure of making the decision. A good many other people, by contrast, need an adviser to force themselves to think; then they can make decisions and act on them with speed, self-confidence, and courage.

This is a reason, by the way, that the number two person in an organization often fails when promoted to the number one position. The top spot requires a decision maker. Strong decision makers often put somebody they trust into the number two spot as their adviser—and in that position the person is outstanding. But in the number one spot, the same person fails. He or she knows what the decision should be but cannot accept the responsibility of actually making it.

Other important questions to ask include, Do I perform well under stress, or do I need a highly structured and predictable environment? Do I work best in a big organization or a small one? Few people work well in all kinds of environments. Again and again, I have seen people who were very successful in large organizations flounder miserably when they moved into smaller ones. And the reverse is equally true.

The conclusion bears repeating: Do not try to change yourself—you are unlikely to succeed. But work hard to improve the way you perform. And try not to take on work you cannot perform or will only perform poorly.

What Are My Values?

To be able to manage yourself, you finally have to ask, What are my values? This is not a question of ethics. With respect to ethics, the rules are the same for everybody, and the test is a simple one. I call it the "mirror test."

In the early years of this century, the most highly respected diplomat of all the great powers was the German ambassador in London. He was clearly destined for great things—to become his country's foreign minister, at least, if not its federal chancellor. Yet in 1906 he abruptly resigned rather than preside over a dinner given by the diplomatic corps for Edward VII. The king was a notorious womanizer and made it clear what kind of dinner he wanted. The ambassador is reported to have said, "I refuse to see a pimp in the mirror in the morning when I shave."

That is the mirror test. Ethics requires that you ask yourself, What kind of person do I want to see in the mirror in the morning? What is ethical behavior in one kind of organization or situation is ethical behavior in another. But ethics is only part of a value system—especially of an organization's value system.

To work in an organization whose value system is unacceptable or incompatible with one's own condemns a person both to frustration and to nonperformance.

Consider the experience of a highly successful human resources executive whose company was acquired by a bigger organization. After the acquisition, she was promoted to do the kind of work she did best, which included selecting people for important positions. The executive deeply believed that a company should hire people for such positions from the outside only after exhausting all the inside possibilities. But her new company believed in first looking outside "to bring in fresh blood." There is something to be said for both approaches—in my experience, the proper one is to do some of both. They are, however, fundamentally incompatible—not as policies but as values. They bespeak different views of the relationship between organizations and people; different views of the responsibility of an organization to its people and their development; and different views of a person's most important contribution to an enterprise. After several years of frustration, the executive quit—at considerable financial loss. Her values and the values of the organization simply were not compatible.

Similarly, whether a pharmaceutical company tries to obtain results by making constant, small improvements or by achieving occasional, highly expensive, and risky "breakthroughs" is not primarily an economic question. The results of either strategy may be pretty much the same. At bottom, there is a conflict between a value system that sees the company's contribution in terms of helping physicians do better what they already do and a value system that is oriented toward making scientific discoveries.

Whether a business should be run for short-term results or with a focus on the long term is likewise a question of values. Financial analysts believe that businesses can be run for both simultaneously. Successful businesspeople know better. To be sure, every company has to produce short-term results. But in any conflict between short-term results and long-term growth, each company will determine its own priority. This is not primarily a disagreement about economics. It is fundamentally a value conflict regarding the function of a business and the responsibility of management.

Value conflicts are not limited to business organizations. One of the fastest-growing pastoral churches in the United States measures success by the number of new parishioners. Its leadership believes that what matters is how many newcomers join the congregation. The Good Lord will then minister to their spiritual needs or at least to the needs of a sufficient percentage. Another pastoral, evangelical church believes that what matters is people's spiritual growth. The church eases out newcomers who join but do not enter into its spiritual life.

Again, this is not a matter of numbers. At first glance, it appears that the second church grows more slowly. But it retains a far larger proportion of newcomers than the first one does. Its growth, in other words, is more solid. This is also not a theological problem, or only secondarily so. It is a problem about values. In a public debate, one pastor argued, "Unless you first come to church, you will never find the gate to the Kingdom of Heaven."

"No," answered the other. "Until you first look for the gate to the Kingdom of Heaven, you don't belong in church."

Organizations, like people, have values. To be effective in an organization, a person's values must be compatible with the organization's values. They do not need to be the same, but they must be close enough to coexist. Otherwise, the person will not only be frustrated but also will not produce results.

A person's strengths and the way that person performs rarely conflict; the two are complementary. But there is sometimes a conflict between a person's values and his or her strengths. What one does well—even very well and successfully—may not fit with one's value system. In that case, the work may not appear to be worth devoting one's life to (or even a substantial portion thereof).

If I may, allow me to interject a personal note. Many years ago, I too had to decide between my values and what I was doing successfully. I was doing very well as a young investment banker in London in the mid-1930s, and the work clearly fit my strengths. Yet I did not see myself making a contribution as an asset manager. People, I realized, were what I valued, and I saw no point in being the richest man in the cemetery. I had no money and no other job prospects. Despite the continuing Depression, I quit—and it was the right thing to do. Values, in other words, are and should be the ultimate test.

Where Do I Belong?

A small number of people know very early where they belong. Mathematicians, musicians, and cooks, for instance, are usually mathematicians, musicians, and cooks by the time they are four or five years old. Physicians usually decide on their careers in their teens, if not earlier. But most people, especially highly gifted people, do not really know where they belong until they are well past their mid-twenties. By that time, however, they should know the answers to the three questions: What are my strengths? How do I perform? and, What are my values? And then they can and should decide where they belong.

Or rather, they should be able to decide where they do *not* belong. The person who has learned that he or she does not perform well in a big organization should have learned to say no to a position in one. The person who has learned that he or she is not a decision maker should have learned to say no to a decision-making assignment. A General Patton (who probably never learned this himself) should have learned to say no to an independent command.

Equally important, knowing the answer to these questions enables a person to say to an opportunity, an offer, or an assignment, "Yes, I will do that. But this is the way I should be doing it. This is the way it should be structured. This is the way the relationships should be. These are the kind of results you should expect from me, and in this time frame, because this is who I am."

Successful careers are not planned. They develop when people are prepared for opportunities because they know their strengths, their method of work, and their values. Knowing where one belongs can transform an ordinary person—hardworking and competent but otherwise mediocre—into an outstanding performer.

What Should I Contribute?

Throughout history, the great majority of people never had to ask the question, What should I contribute? They were told what to contribute, and their tasks were dictated either by the work itself—as it was for the peasant or artisan—or by a master or a mistress—as it was for domestic servants. And until very recently, it was taken for granted that most people were subordinates who did as they were told. Even in the 1950s and 1960s, the new knowledge workers (the so-called organization men) looked to their company's personnel department to plan their careers.

Then in the late 1960s, no one wanted to be told what to do any longer. Young men and women began to ask, What do *I* want to do? And what they heard was that the way to contribute was to "do your own thing." But this solution was as wrong as the organization men's had been. Very few of the people who believed that doing one's own thing would lead to contribution, self-fulfillment, and success achieved any of the three.

But still, there is no return to the old answer of doing what you are told or assigned to do. Knowledge workers in particular have to learn to ask a question that has not been asked before: What *should* my contribution be? To answer it, they must address three distinct elements: What does the situation require? Given my strengths, my way of performing, and my values, how can I make the greatest contribution to what needs to be done? And finally, What results have to be achieved to make a difference?

Consider the experience of a newly appointed hospital administrator. The hospital was big and prestigious, but it had been coasting on its reputation for 30 years. The new administrator decided that his contribution should be to establish a standard of excellence in one important area within two years. He chose to focus on the emergency room, which was big, visible, and sloppy. He decided that every patient who came into the ER had to be seen by a qualified nurse within 60 seconds. Within 12 months, the hospital's emergency room had become a model for all hospitals in the United States, and within another two years, the whole hospital had been transformed.

As this example suggests, it is rarely possible—or even particularly fruitful—to look too far ahead. A plan can usually cover no more than 18 months and still be reasonably clear and specific. So the question in most cases should be, Where and how can I achieve results that will make a difference within the next year and a half? The answer must balance several things. First, the results should be hard to achieve—they should require "stretching," to use the current buzzword. But also, they should be within reach. To aim at results that cannot be achieved—or that can be only under the most unlikely circumstances—is not being ambitious; it is being foolish. Second, the results should be meaningful. They should make a difference. Finally, results should be visible and, if at all possible, measurable. From this will come a course of action: what to do, where and how to start, and what goals and deadlines to set.

Responsibility for Relationships

Very few people work by themselves and achieve results by themselves—a few great artists, a few great scientists, a few great athletes. Most people work with others and are effective with other people. That is true whether they are members of an organization or independently employed. Managing yourself requires taking responsibility for relationships. This has two parts.

The first is to accept the fact that other people are as much individuals as you yourself are. They perversely insist on behaving like human beings. This means that they too have their strengths; they too have their ways of getting things done; they too have their values. To be effective, therefore, you have to know the strengths, the performance modes, and the values of your coworkers.

That sounds obvious, but few people pay attention to it. Typical is the person who was trained to write reports in his or her first assignment because that boss was a reader. Even if the next boss is a listener, the person goes on writing reports that, invariably, produce no results. Invariably the boss will think the employee is stupid, incompetent, and lazy, and he or she will fail. But that could have been avoided if the employee had only looked at the new boss and analyzed how *this* boss performs.

Bosses are neither a title on the organization chart nor a "function." They are individuals and are entitled to do their work in the way they do it best. It is incumbent on the people who work with them to observe them, to find out how they work, and to adapt themselves to what makes their bosses most effective. This, in fact, is the secret of "managing" the boss.

The same holds true for all your coworkers. Each works his or her way, not your way. And each is entitled to work in his or her way. What matters is whether they perform and what their values are. As for how they perform—each is likely to do it differently. The first secret of effectiveness is to understand the people you work with and depend on so that you can make use of their strengths, their ways of working, and their values. Working relationships are as much based on the people as they are on the work.

The second part of relationship responsibility is taking responsibility for communication. Whenever I, or any other consultant, start to work with an organization, the first thing I hear about are all the personality conflicts. Most of these arise from the fact that people do not know what other people are doing and how they do their work, or what contribution the other people are concentrating on and what results they expect. And the reason they do not know is that they have not asked and therefore have not been told.

This failure to ask reflects human stupidity less than it reflects human history. Until recently, it was unnecessary to tell any of these things to anybody. In the medieval city, everyone in a district plied the same trade. In the countryside, everyone in a valley planted the same crop as soon as the frost was out of the ground. Even those few people who did things that were not "common" worked alone, so they did not have to tell anyone what they were doing.

Today the great majority of people work with others who have different tasks and responsibilities. The marketing vice president may have come out of sales and know everything about sales, but she knows nothing about the things she has never done—pricing, advertising, packaging, and the like. So the people who do these things must make sure that the marketing vice president understands what they are trying to do, why they are trying to do it, how they are going to do it, and what results to expect.

If the marketing vice president does not understand what these high-grade knowledge specialists are doing, it is primarily their fault, not hers. They have not educated her. Conversely, it is the marketing vice president's responsibility to make sure that all of her coworkers understand how she looks at marketing: what her goals are, how she works, and what she expects of herself and of each one of them.

Even people who understand the importance of taking responsibility for relationships often do not communicate sufficiently with their associates. They are afraid of being thought presumptuous or inquisitive or stupid. They are wrong. Whenever someone goes to his or her associates and says, "This is what I am good at. This is how I work. These are my values. This is the contribution I plan to concentrate on and the results I should be expected to deliver," the response is always, "This is most helpful. But why didn't you tell me earlier?"

And one gets the same reaction—without exception, in my experience—if one continues by asking, "And what do I need to know about your strengths, how you perform, your values, and your proposed contribution?" In fact, knowledge workers should request this of everyone with whom they work, whether as subordinate, superior, colleague, or team member. And again, whenever this is done, the reaction is always, "Thanks for asking me. But why didn't you ask me earlier?"

Organizations are no longer built on force but on trust. The existence of trust between people does not necessarily mean that they like one another. It means that they understand one another. Taking responsibility for relationships is therefore an absolute necessity. It is a duty. Whether one is a member of the organization, a consultant to it, a supplier, or a distributor, one owes that responsibility to all one's coworkers: those whose work one depends on as well as those who depend on one's own work.

The Second Half of Your Life

When work for most people meant manual labor, there was no need to worry about the second half of your life. You simply kept on doing what you had always done. And if you were lucky enough to survive 40 years of hard work in the mill or on the railroad, you were quite happy to spend the rest of your life doing nothing. Today, however, most work is knowledge work, and knowledge workers are not "finished" after 40 years on the job, they are merely bored.

We hear a great deal of talk about the midlife crisis of the executive. It is mostly boredom. At 45, most executives have reached the peak of their business careers, and they know it. After 20 years of doing very much the same kind of work, they are very good at their jobs. But they are not learning or contributing or deriving challenge and satisfaction from the job. And yet they are still likely to face another 20 if not 25 years of work. That is why managing oneself increasingly leads one to begin a second career.

There are three ways to develop a second career. The first is actually to start one. Often this takes nothing more than moving from one kind of organization to another: the divisional controller in a large corporation, for instance, becomes the controller of a medium-sized hospital. But there are also growing numbers of people who move into different lines of work altogether: the business executive or government official who enters the ministry at 45, for instance; or the midlevel manager who leaves corporate life after 20 years to attend law school and become a small-town attorney.

We will see many more second careers undertaken by people who have achieved modest success in their first jobs. Such people have substantial skills, and they know how to work. They need a community—the house is empty with the children gone—and they need income as well. But above all, they need challenge.

The second way to prepare for the second half of your life is to develop a parallel career. Many people who are very successful in their first careers stay in the work they have been doing, either on a full-time or part-time or consulting basis. But in addition, they create a parallel job, usually in a nonprofit organization, that takes another ten hours of work a week. They might take over the administration of their church, for instance, or the presidency of the local Girl Scouts council. They might run the battered women's shelter, work as a children's librarian for the local public library, sit on the school board, and so on.

Finally, there are the social entrepreneurs. These are usually people who have been very successful in their first careers. They love their work, but it no longer challenges them. In many cases they keep on doing what they have been doing all along but spend less and less of their time on it. They also start another activity, usually a nonprofit. My friend Bob Buford, for example, built a very successful television company that he still runs. But he has also founded and built a successful nonprofit organization that works with Protestant churches, and he is building another to teach social entrepreneurs how to manage their own nonprofit ventures while still running their original businesses.

People who manage the second half of their lives may always be a minority. The majority may "retire on the job" and count the years until their actual retirement. But it is this minority, the men and women who see a long working-life expectancy as an opportunity both for themselves and for society, who will become leaders and models.

There is one prerequisite for managing the second half of your life: You must begin long before you enter it. When it first became clear 30 years ago that working-life expectancies were lengthening very fast, many observers (including myself) believed that retired people would increasingly become volunteers for nonprofit institutions. That has not happened. If one does not begin to volunteer before one is 40 or so, one will not volunteer once past 60.

Similarly, all the social entrepreneurs I know began to work in their chosen second enterprise long before they reached their peak in their original business. Consider the example of a successful lawyer, the legal counsel to a large corporation, who has started a venture to establish model schools in his state. He began to do volunteer legal work for the schools when he was around 35. He was elected to the school board at age 40. At age 50, when he had amassed a fortune, he started his own enterprise to build and to run model schools. He is, however, still working nearly full-time as the lead counsel in the company he helped found as a young lawyer.

There is another reason to develop a second major interest, and to develop it early. No one can expect to live very long without experiencing a serious setback in his or her life or work. There is the competent engineer who is passed over for promotion at age 45. There is the competent college professor who realizes at age 42 that she will never get a professorship at a big university, even though she may be fully qualified for it. There are tragedies in one's family life: the breakup of one's marriage or the loss of a child. At such times, a second major interest—not just a hobby—may make all the difference. The engineer, for example, now knows that he has not been very successful in his job. But in his outside activity—as church treasurer, for example—he is a success. One's family may break up, but in that outside activity there is still a community.

In a society in which success has become so terribly important, having options will become increasingly vital. Historically, there was no such thing as "success." The overwhelming majority of people did not expect anything but to stay in their "proper station," as an old English prayer has it. The only mobility was downward mobility.

In a knowledge society, however, we expect everyone to be a success. This is clearly an impossibility. For a great many people, there is at best an absence of failure. Wherever there is success, there has to be failure. And then it is vitally important for the individual, and equally for the individual's family, to have an area in which he or she can contribute, make a difference, and be *somebody*. That means finding a second area—whether in a second career, a parallel career, or a social venture—that offers an opportunity for being a leader, for being respected, for being a success.

The challenges of managing oneself may seem obvious, if not elementary. And the answers may seem self-evident to the point of appearing naïve. But managing oneself requires new and unprecedented things from the individual, and especially from the knowledge worker. In effect, managing oneself demands that each knowledge worker think and behave like a chief executive officer. Further, the shift from manual workers who do as they are told to knowledge workers who have to manage themselves profoundly challenges social structure. Every existing society, even the most individualistic one, takes two things for granted, if only subconsciously: that organizations outlive workers, and that most people stay put.

But today the opposite is true. Knowledge workers outlive organizations, and they are mobile. The need to manage oneself is therefore creating a revolution in human affairs.

Originally published in January 1999. Reprint R0501K

Management Time: Who's Got the Monkey?

by William Oncken, Jr., and Donald L. Wass

WHY IS IT THAT MANAGERS are typically running out of time while their subordinates are typically running out of work? Here we shall explore the meaning of management time as it relates to the inter-action between managers and their bosses, their peers, and their subordinates.

Specifically, we shall deal with three kinds of management time:

Boss-imposed time—used to accomplish those activities that the boss requires and that the manager cannot disregard without direct and swift penalty.

System-imposed time—used to accommodate requests from peers for active support. Neglecting these requests will also result in penalties, though not always as direct or swift.

Self-imposed time—used to do those things that the manager originates or agrees to do. A certain portion of this kind of time, however, will be taken by subordinates and is called *subordinate-imposed time*. The remaining portion will be the manager's own and is called *discretionary time*. Self-imposed time is not subject to penalty since neither the boss nor the system can discipline the manager for not doing what they didn't know he had intended to do in the first place.

To accommodate those demands, managers need to control the timing and the content of what they do. Since what their bosses and the system impose on them are subject to penalty, managers cannot tamper with those requirements. Thus their self-imposed time becomes their major area of concern.

Managers should try to increase the discretionary component of their self-imposed time by minimizing or doing away with the subordinate component. They will then use the added increment to get better control over their boss-imposed and system-imposed activities. Most managers spend much more time dealing with subordinates' problems than they even faintly realize. Hence we shall use the monkey-on-the-back metaphor to examine how subordinate-imposed time comes into being and what the superior can do about it.

Where Is the Monkey?

Let us imagine that a manager is walking down the hall and that he notices one of his subordinates, Jones, coming his way. When the two meet, Jones greets the manager with, "Good morning. By the way, we've got a problem. You see . . . ." As Jones continues, the manager recognizes in this problem the two characteristics common to all the problems his subordinates gratuitously bring to his attention. Namely, the manager knows (a) enough to get involved, but (b) not enough to make the on-the-spot decision expected of him. Eventually, the manager says, "So glad you brought this up. I'm in a rush right now. Meanwhile, let me think about it, and I'll let you know." Then he and Jones part company.

Let us analyze what just happened. Before the two of them met, on whose back was the "monkey"? The subordinate's. After they parted, on whose back was it? The manager's. Subordinate-imposed time begins the moment a monkey successfully leaps from the back of a subordinate to the back of his or her superior and does not end until the monkey is returned to its proper owner for care and feeding. In accepting the monkey, the manager has voluntarily assumed a position subordinate to his subordinate. That is, he has allowed

Idea in Brief

You're racing down the hall. An employee stops you and says, "We've got a problem." You assume you should get involved but can't make an on-the-spot decision. You say, "Let me think about it."

You've just allowed a "monkey" to leap from your subordinate's back to yours. *You're* now working for your *subordinate*. Take on enough monkeys, and you won't have time to handle your *real* job: fulfilling your own boss's mandates and helping peers generate business results.

How to avoid accumulating monkeys? Develop your subordinates' initiative, say Oncken and Wass. For example, when an employee tries to hand you a problem, clarify whether he should: recommend and implement a solution, take action then brief you immediately, or act and report the outcome at a regular update.

When you encourage employees to handle their own monkeys, they acquire new skills—and you liberate time to do your own job.

Jones to make him her subordinate by doing two things a subordinate is generally expected to do for a boss—the manager has accepted a responsibility from his subordinate, and the manager has promised her a progress report.

The subordinate, to make sure the manager does not miss this point, will later stick her head in the manager's office and cheerily query, "How's it coming?" (This is called supervision.)

Or let us imagine in concluding a conference with Johnson, another subordinate, the manager's parting words are, "Fine. Send me a memo on that."

Let us analyze this one. The monkey is now on the subordinate's back because the next move is his, but it is poised for a leap. Watch that monkey. Johnson dutifully writes the requested memo and drops it in his out-basket. Shortly thereafter, the manager plucks it from his in-basket and reads it. Whose move is it now? The manager's. If he does not make that move soon, he will get a follow-up memo from the subordinate. (This is another form of supervision.) The longer the manager delays, the more frustrated the subordinate will become (he'll be spinning his wheels) and the more guilty the

Idea in Practice

How to return monkeys to their proper owners? Oncken, Wass, and Steven Covey (in an afterword to this classic article) offer these suggestions.

Make Appointments to Deal with Monkeys

Avoid discussing any monkey on an ad hoc basis—for example, when you pass a subordinate in the hallway. You won't convey the proper seriousness. Instead, schedule an appointment to discuss the issue.

Specify Level of Initiative

Your employees can exercise five levels of initiative in handling on-the-job problems. From lowest to highest, the levels are:

1. Wait until told what to do.

2. Ask what to do.

3. Recommend an action, then with your approval, implement it.

4. Take independent action but advise you at once.

5. Take independent action and update you through routine procedure.

When an employee brings a problem to you, outlaw use of level 1 or 2. Agree on and assign level 3, 4, or 5 to the monkey. Take no more than 15 minutes to discuss the problem.

Agree on a Status Update

After deciding how to proceed, agree on a time and place when the employee will give you a progress report.

Examine Your Own Motives

Some managers secretly worry that if they encourage subordinates to take more initiative, they'll appear less strong, more vulnerable, and less useful. Instead, cultivate an inward sense of security that frees you to relinquish direct control and support employees' growth.

Develop Employees' Skills

Employees try to hand off monkeys when they lack the desire or ability to handle them. Help employees develop needed problem-solving skills. It's initially more time consuming than tackling problems yourself—but it saves time in the long run.

Foster Trust

Developing employees' initiative requires a trusting relationship between you and your subordinates. If they're afraid of failing, they'll keep bringing their monkeys to you rather than working to solve their own problems. To promote trust, reassure them it's safe to make mistakes.

manager will feel (his backlog of subordinate-imposed time will be mounting).

Or suppose once again that at a meeting with a third subordinate, Smith, the manager agrees to provide all the necessary backing for a public relations proposal he has just asked Smith to develop. The manager's parting words to her are, "Just let me know how I can help."

Now let us analyze this. Again the monkey is initially on the subordinate's back. But for how long? Smith realizes that she cannot let the manager "know" until her proposal has the manager's approval. And from experience, she also realizes that her proposal will likely be sitting in the manager's briefcase for weeks before he eventually gets to it. Who's really got the monkey? Who will be checking up on whom? Wheel spinning and bottlenecking are well on their way again.

A fourth subordinate, Reed, has just been transferred from another part of the company so that he can launch and eventually manage a newly created business venture. The manager has said they should get together soon to hammer out a set of objectives for the new job, adding, "I will draw up an initial draft for discussion with you."

Let us analyze this one, too. The subordinate has the new job (by formal assignment) and the full responsibility (by formal delegation), but the manager has the next move. Until he makes it, he will have the monkey, and the subordinate will be immobilized.

Why does all of this happen? Because in each instance the manager and the subordinate assume at the outset, wittingly or unwittingly, that the matter under consideration is a joint problem. The monkey in each case begins its career astride both their backs. All it has to do is move the wrong leg, and—presto!—the subordinate deftly disappears. The manager is thus left with another acquisition for his menagerie. Of course, monkeys can be trained not to move the wrong leg. But it is easier to prevent them from straddling backs in the first place.

Who Is Working for Whom?

Let us suppose that these same four subordinates are so thoughtful and considerate of their superior's time that they take pains to allow no more than three monkeys to leap from each of their backs to his in any one day. In a five-day week, the manager will have picked up 60 screaming monkeys—far too many to do anything about them individually. So he spends his subordinate-imposed time juggling his "priorities."

Late Friday afternoon, the manager is in his office with the door closed for privacy so he can contemplate the situation, while his subordinates are waiting outside to get their last chance before the weekend to remind him that he will have to "fish or cut bait." Imagine what they are saying to one another about the manager as they wait: "What a bottleneck. He just can't make up his mind. How anyone ever got that high up in our company without being able to make a decision we'll never know."

Worst of all, the reason the manager cannot make any of these "next moves" is that his time is almost entirely eaten up by meeting his own boss-imposed and system-imposed requirements. To control those tasks, he needs discretionary time that is in turn denied him when he is preoccupied with all these monkeys. The manager is caught in a vicious circle. But time is a-wasting (an understatement). The manager calls his secretary on the intercom and instructs her to tell his subordinates that he won't be able to see them until Monday morning. At 7 PM, he drives home, intending with firm resolve to return to the office tomorrow to get caught up over the weekend. He returns bright and early the next day only to see, on the nearest green of the golf course across from his office window, a foursome. Guess who?

That does it. He now knows who is really working for whom. Moreover, he now sees that if he actually accomplishes during this weekend what he came to accomplish, his subordinates' morale will go up so sharply that they will each raise the limit on the number of monkeys they will let jump from their backs to his. In short, he now sees, with the clarity of a revelation on a mountaintop, that the more he gets caught up, the more he will fall behind.

He leaves the office with the speed of a person running away from a plague. His plan? To get caught up on something else he hasn't had time for in years: a weekend with his family. (This is one of the many varieties of discretionary time.)

Sunday night he enjoys ten hours of sweet, untroubled slumber, because he has clear-cut plans for Monday. He is going to get rid of his subordinate-imposed time. In exchange, he will get an equal amount of discretionary time, part of which he will spend with his subordinates to make sure that they learn the difficult but rewarding managerial art called "The Care and Feeding of Monkeys."

The manager will also have plenty of discretionary time left over for getting control of the timing and the content not only of his boss-imposed time but also of his system-imposed time. It may take months, but compared with the way things have been, the rewards will be enormous. His ultimate objective is to manage his time.

Getting Rid of the Monkeys

The manager returns to the office Monday morning just late enough so that his four subordinates have collected outside his office waiting to see him about their monkeys. He calls them in one by one. The purpose of each interview is to take a monkey, place it on the desk between them, and figure out together how the next move might conceivably be the subordinate's. For certain monkeys, that will take some doing. The subordinate's next move may be so elusive that the manager may decide—just for now—merely to let the monkey sleep on the subordinate's back overnight and have him or her return with it at an appointed time the next morning to continue the joint quest for a more substantive move by the subordinate. (Monkeys sleep just as soundly overnight on subordinates' backs as they do on superiors'.)

As each subordinate leaves the office, the manager is rewarded by the sight of a monkey leaving his office on the subordinate's back. For the next 24 hours, the subordinate will not be waiting for the manager; instead, the manager will be waiting for the subordinate.

Later, as if to remind himself that there is no law against his engaging in a constructive exercise in the interim, the manager strolls by the subordinate's office, sticks his head in the door, and cheerily asks, "How's it coming?" (The time consumed in doing this is discretionary for the manager and boss imposed for the subordinate.)

Making Time for Gorillas

by Stephen R. Covey

WHEN BILL ONCKEN WROTE this article in 1974, managers were in a terrible bind. They were desperate for a way to free up their time, but command and control was the status quo. Managers felt they weren't allowed to empower their subordinates to make decisions. Too dangerous. Too risky. That's why Oncken's message—give the monkey back to its rightful owner—involved a critically important paradigm shift. Many managers working today owe him a debt of gratitude.

It is something of an understatement, however, to observe that much has changed since Oncken's radical recommendation. Command and control as a management philosophy is all but dead, and "empowerment" is the word of the day in most organizations trying to thrive in global, intensely competitive markets. But command and control stubbornly remains a common practice. Management thinkers and executives have discovered in the last decade that bosses cannot just give a monkey back to their subordinates and then merrily get on with their own business. Empowering subordinates is hard and complicated work.

The reason: when you give problems back to subordinates to solve themselves, you have to be sure that they have both the desire and the ability to do so. As every executive knows, that isn't always the case. Enter a whole new set of problems. Empowerment often means you have to develop people, which is initially much more time consuming than solving the problem on your own.

Just as important, empowerment can only thrive when the whole organization buys into it—when formal systems and the informal culture support it. Managers need to be rewarded for delegating decisions and developing people. Otherwise, the degree of real empowerment in an organization will vary according to the beliefs and practices of individual managers.

But perhaps the most important lesson about empowerment is that effective delegation—the kind Oncken advocated—depends on a trusting relationship between a manager and his subordinate. Oncken's message may have been ahead of his time, but what he suggested was still a fairly dictatorial solution. He basically told bosses, "Give the problem back!" Today, we know that this approach by itself is too authoritarian. To delegate effectively, executives need to establish a running dialogue with subordinates. They need to establish a partnership. After all, if subordinates are afraid of failing in front of their boss, they'll keep coming back for help rather than truly take initiative.

Oncken's article also doesn't address an aspect of delegation that has greatly interested me during the past two decades—that many managers are actually *eager* to take on their subordinates' monkeys. Nearly all the managers I talk with agree that their people are underutilized in their present jobs. But even some of the most successful, seemingly self-assured executives have talked about how hard it is to give up control to their subordinates.

I've come to attribute that eagerness for control to a common, deep-seated belief that rewards in life are scarce and fragile. Whether they learn it from their family, school, or athletics, many people establish an identity by comparing themselves with others. When they see others gain power, information, money, or recognition, for instance, they experience what the psychologist Abraham Maslow called "a feeling of deficiency"—a sense that something is being taken from them. That makes it hard for them to be genuinely happy about the success of others—even of their loved ones. Oncken implies that managers can easily give back or refuse monkeys, but many managers may subconsciously fear that a subordinate taking the initiative will make them appear a little less strong and a little more vulnerable.

How, then, do managers develop the inward security, the mentality of "abundance," that would enable them to relinquish control and seek the growth and development of those around them? The work I've done with numerous organizations suggests that managers who live with integrity according to a principle-based value system are most likely to sustain an empowering style of leadership.

Given the times in which he wrote, it was no wonder that Oncken's message resonated with managers. But it was reinforced by Oncken's wonderful gift for storytelling. I got to know Oncken on the speaker's circuit in the 1970s, and I was always impressed by how he dramatized his ideas in colorful detail. Like the Dilbert comic strip, Oncken had a tongue-in-cheek style that got to the core of managers' frustrations and made them want to take back control of their time. And the monkey on your back wasn't just a metaphor for Oncken—it was his personal symbol. I saw him several times walking through airports with a stuffed monkey on his shoulder.

I'm not surprised that his article is one of the two best-selling HBR articles ever. Even with all we know about empowerment, its vivid message is even more important and relevant now than it was 25 years ago. Indeed, Oncken's insight is a basis for my own work on time management, in which I have people categorize their activities according to urgency and importance. I've heard from executives again and again that half or more of their time is spent on matters that are urgent but not important. They're trapped in an endless

(continued)

cycle of dealing with other people's monkeys, yet they're reluctant to help those people take their own initiative. As a result, they're often too busy to spend the time they need on the real gorillas in their organization. Oncken's article remains a powerful wake-up call for managers who need to delegate effectively.

Stephen R. Covey is vice chairman of the Franklin Covey Company, a global provider of leadership development and productivity services and products.

When the subordinate (with the monkey on his or her back) and the manager meet at the appointed hour the next day, the manager explains the ground rules in words to this effect:

"At no time while I am helping you with this or any other problem will your problem become my problem. The instant your problem becomes mine, you no longer have a problem. I cannot help a person who hasn't got a problem.

"When this meeting is over, the problem will leave this office exactly the way it came in—on your back. You may ask my help at any appointed time, and we will make a joint determination of what the next move will be and which of us will make it.

"In those rare instances where the next move turns out to be mine, you and I will determine it together. I will not make any move alone."

The manager follows this same line of thought with each subordinate until about 11 AM, when he realizes that he doesn't have to close his door. His monkeys are gone. They will return—but by appointment only. His calendar will assure this.

Transferring the Initiative

What we have been driving at in this monkey-on-the-back analogy is that managers can transfer initiative back to their subordinates and keep it there. We have tried to highlight a truism as obvious as it is subtle: namely, before developing initiative in subordinates, the manager must see to it that they *have* the initiative. Once the manager takes it back, he will no longer have it and he can kiss his discretionary time good-bye. It will all revert to subordinate-imposed time.

Nor can the manager and the subordinate effectively have the same initiative at the same time. The opener, "Boss, we've got a problem," implies this duality and represents, as noted earlier, a monkey astride two backs, which is a very bad way to start a monkey on its career. Let us, therefore, take a few moments to examine what we call "The Anatomy of Managerial Initiative."

There are five degrees of initiative that the manager can exercise in relation to the boss and to the system:

1. wait until told (lowest initiative);

2. ask what to do;

3. recommend, then take resulting action;

4. act, but advise at once;

5. and act on own, then routinely report (highest initiative).

Clearly, the manager should be professional enough not to indulge in initiatives 1 and 2 in relation either to the boss or to the system. A manager who uses initiative 1 has no control over either the timing or the content of boss-imposed or system-imposed time and thereby forfeits any right to complain about what he or she is told to do or when. The manager who uses initiative 2 has control over the timing but not over the content. Initiatives 3, 4, and 5 leave the manager in control of both, with the greatest amount of control being exercised at level 5.

In relation to subordinates, the manager's job is twofold. First, to outlaw the use of initiatives 1 and 2, thus giving subordinates no choice but to learn and master "Completed Staff Work." Second, to see that for each problem leaving his or her office there is an agreed-upon level of initiative assigned to it, in addition to an agreed-upon time and place for the next manager-subordinate conference. The latter should be duly noted on the manager's calendar.

The Care and Feeding of Monkeys

To further clarify our analogy between the monkey on the back and the processes of assigning and controlling, we shall refer briefly to the manager's appointment schedule, which calls for five hard-and-fast rules governing the "Care and Feeding of Monkeys." (Violation of these rules will cost discretionary time.)

Rule 1

Monkeys should be fed or shot. Otherwise, they will starve to death, and the manager will waste valuable time on postmortems or attempted resurrections.

Rule 2

The monkey population should be kept below the maximum number the manager has time to feed. Subordinates will find time to work as many monkeys as he or she finds time to feed, but no more. It shouldn't take more than five to 15 minutes to feed a properly maintained monkey.

Rule 3

Monkeys should be fed by appointment only. The manager should not have to hunt down starving monkeys and feed them on a catch-as-catch-can basis.

Rule 4

Monkeys should be fed face-to-face or by telephone, but never by mail. (Remember—with mail, the next move will be the manager's.) Documentation may add to the feeding process, but it cannot take the place of feeding.

Rule 5

Every monkey should have an assigned next feeding time and degree of initiative. These may be revised at any time by mutual consent but never allowed to become vague or indefinite. Otherwise, the monkey will either starve to death or wind up on the manager's back.

"Get control over the timing and content of what you do" is appropriate advice for managing time. The first order of business is for the manager to enlarge his or her discretionary time by eliminating subordinate-imposed time. The second is for the manager to use a portion of this newfound discretionary time to see to it that each subordinate actually has the initiative and applies it. The third is for the manager to use another portion of the increased discretionary time to get and keep control of the timing and content of both boss-imposed and system-imposed time. All these steps will increase the manager's leverage and enable the value of each hour spent in managing management time to multiply without theoretical limit.

Originally published in November 1999. Reprint 99609

How Resilience Works

by Diane L. Coutu

WHEN I BEGAN MY CAREER IN JOURNALISM—I was a reporter at a national magazine in those days—there was a man I'll call Claus Schmidt. He was in his mid-fifties, and to my impressionable eyes, he was the quintessential newsman: cynical at times, but unrelentingly curious and full of life, and often hilariously funny in a sandpaper-dry kind of way. He churned out hard-hitting cover stories and features with a speed and elegance I could only dream of. It always astounded me that he was never promoted to managing editor.

But people who knew Claus better than I did thought of him not just as a great newsman but as a quintessential survivor, someone who had endured in an environment often hostile to talent. He had lived through at least three major changes in the magazine's leadership, losing most of his best friends and colleagues on the way. At home, two of his children succumbed to incurable illnesses, and a third was killed in a traffic accident. Despite all this—or maybe because of it—he milled around the newsroom day after day, mentoring the cub reporters, talking about the novels he was writing—always looking forward to what the future held for him.

Why do some people suffer real hardships and not falter? Claus Schmidt could have reacted very differently. We've all seen that happen: One person cannot seem to get the confidence back after a layoff; another, persistently depressed, takes a few years off from life after her divorce. The question we would all like answered is, Why? What exactly is that quality of resilience that carries people through life?

It's a question that has fascinated me ever since I first learned of the Holocaust survivors in elementary school. In college, and later in my studies as an affiliate scholar at the Boston Psychoanalytic Society and Institute, I returned to the subject. For the past several months, however, I have looked on it with a new urgency, for it seems to me that the terrorism, war, and recession of recent months have made understanding resilience more important than ever. I have considered both the nature of individual resilience and what makes some organizations as a whole more resilient than others. Why do some people and some companies buckle under pressure? And what makes others bend and ultimately bounce back?

My exploration has taught me much about resilience, although it's a subject none of us will ever understand fully. Indeed, resilience is one of the great puzzles of human nature, like creativity or the religious instinct. But in sifting through psychological research and in reflecting on the many stories of resilience I've heard, I have seen a little more deeply into the hearts and minds of people like Claus Schmidt and, in doing so, looked more deeply into the human psyche as well.

The Buzz About Resilience

Resilience is a hot topic in business these days. Not long ago, I was talking to a senior partner at a respected consulting firm about how to land the very best MBAs—the name of the game in that particular industry. The partner, Daniel Savageau (not his real name), ticked off a long list of qualities his firm sought in its hires: intelligence, ambition, integrity, analytic ability, and so on. "What about resilience?" I asked. "Well, that's very popular right now," he said. "It's the new buzzword. Candidates even tell us they're resilient; they volunteer the information. But frankly, they're just too young to know that about themselves. Resilience is something you realize you have *after* the fact."

Idea in Brief

These are dark days: people are losing jobs, taking pay cuts, suffering foreclosure on their homes. Some of them are snapping—sinking into depression or suffering a permanent loss of confidence.

But others are snapping back; for example, taking advantage of a layoff to build a new career. What carries them through tough times? Resilience.

Resilient people possess three defining characteristics: They coolly accept the harsh realities facing them. They find meaning in terrible times. And they have an uncanny ability to improvise, making do with whatever's at hand.

In deep recessions, resilience becomes more important than ever. Fortunately, you can learn to be resilient.

"But if you could, would you test for it?" I asked. "Does it matter in business?"

Savageau paused. He's a man in his late forties and a success personally and professionally. Yet it hadn't been a smooth ride to the top. He'd started his life as a poor French Canadian in Woonsocket, Rhode Island, and had lost his father at six. He lucked into a football scholarship but was kicked out of Boston University twice for drinking. He turned his life around in his twenties, married, divorced, remarried, and raised five children. Along the way, he made and lost two fortunes before helping to found the consulting firm he now runs. "Yes, it does matter," he said at last. "In fact, it probably matters more than any of the usual things we look for." In the course of reporting this article, I heard the same assertion time and again. As Dean Becker, the president and CEO of Adaptiv Learning Systems, a four-year-old company in King of Prussia, Pennsylvania, that develops and delivers programs about resilience training, puts it: "More than education, more than experience, more than training, a person's level of resilience will determine who succeeds and who fails. That's true in the cancer ward, it's true in the Olympics, and it's true in the boardroom."

Academic research into resilience started about 40 years ago with pioneering studies by Norman Garmezy, now a professor emeritus at the University of Minnesota in Minneapolis. After studying why

Idea in Practice

Resilience can help you survive and recover from even the most brutal experiences. To cultivate resilience, apply these practices.

Face Down Reality

Instead of slipping into denial to cope with hardship, take a sober, down-to-earth view of the reality of your situation. You'll prepare yourself to act in ways that enable you to endure—training yourself to survive before the fact.

> *Example:* Admiral Jim Stockdale survived being held prisoner and tortured by the Vietcong in part by accepting he could be held for a long time. (He was held for eight years.) Those who didn't make it out of the camps kept optimistically assuming they'd be released

on shorter timetables—by Christmas, by Easter, by the Fourth of July. "I think they all died of broken hearts," Stockdale said.

Search for Meaning

When hard times strike, resist any impulse to view yourself as a victim and to cry, "Why me?" Rather, devise constructs about your suffering to create meaning for yourself and others. You'll build bridges from your present-day ordeal to a fuller, better future. Those bridges will make the present manageable, by removing the sense that the present is overwhelming.

> *Example:* Austrian psychiatrist and Auschwitz survivor Victor Frankl realized that to survive

many children of schizophrenic parents did not suffer psychological illness as a result of growing up with them, he concluded that a certain quality of resilience played a greater role in mental health than anyone had previously suspected.

Today, theories abound about what makes resilience. Looking at Holocaust victims, Maurice Vanderpol, a former president of the Boston Psychoanalytic Society and Institute, found that many of the healthy survivors of concentration camps had what he calls a "plastic shield." The shield was comprised of several factors, including a sense of humor. Often the humor was black, but nonetheless it provided a critical sense of perspective. Other core characteristics that helped included the ability to form attachments to others and the possession of an inner psychological space that protected the survivors from the intrusions of abusive others. Research about other the camp, he had to find some purpose. He did so by imagining himself giving a lecture after the war on the psychology of the concentration camp to help outsiders understand what he had been through. By creating concrete goals for himself, he rose above the sufferings of the moment.

Continually Improvise

When disaster hits, be inventive. Make the most of what you have, putting resources to unfamiliar uses and imagining possibilities others don't see.

Example: Mike founded a business with his friend Paul, selling educational materials to schools, businesses, and consulting firms. When a recession hit, they lost many core clients. Paul went through a bitter divorce, suffered a depression, and couldn't work. When Mike offered to buy him out, Paul slapped him with a lawsuit claiming Mike was trying to steal the business.

Mike kept the company going any way he could—going into joint ventures to sell English-language training materials to Russian and Chinese competitors, publishing newsletters for clients, and even writing video scripts for competitors. The lawsuit was eventually settled in his favor, and he had a new and much more solid business than the one he started out with.

groups uncovered different qualities associated with resilience. The Search Institute, a Minneapolis-based nonprofit organization that focuses on resilience and youth, found that the more resilient kids have an uncanny ability to get adults to help them out. Still other research showed that resilient inner-city youth often have talents such as athletic abilities that attract others to them.

Many of the early theories about resilience stressed the role of genetics. Some people are just born resilient, so the arguments went. There's some truth to that, of course, but an increasing body of empirical evidence shows that resilience—whether in children, survivors of concentration camps, or businesses back from the brink—can be learned. For example, George Vaillant, the director of the Study of Adult Development at Harvard Medical School in Boston, observes that within various groups studied during a 60-year period, some people became markedly more resilient over their lifetimes. Other psychologists claim that unresilient people more easily develop resiliency skills than those with head starts.

Most of the resilience theories I encountered in my research make good common sense. But I also observed that almost all the theories overlap in three ways. Resilient people, they posit, possess three characteristics: a staunch acceptance of reality; a deep belief, often buttressed by strongly held values, that life is meaningful; and an uncanny ability to improvise. You can bounce back from hardship with just one or two of these qualities, but you will only be truly resilient with all three. These three characteristics hold true for resilient organizations as well. Let's take a look at each of them in turn.

Facing Down Reality

A common belief about resilience is that it stems from an optimistic nature. That's true but only as long as such optimism doesn't distort your sense of reality. In extremely adverse situations, rose-colored thinking can actually spell disaster. This point was made poignantly to me by management researcher and writer Jim Collins, who happened upon this concept while researching *Good to Great*, his book on how companies transform themselves out of mediocrity. Collins had a hunch (an exactly wrong hunch) that resilient companies were filled with optimistic people. He tried out that idea on Admiral Jim Stockdale, who was held prisoner and tortured by the Vietcong for eight years.

Collins recalls: "I asked Stockdale: 'Who didn't make it out of the camps?' And he said, 'Oh, that's easy. It was the optimists. They were the ones who said we were going to be out by Christmas. And then they said we'd be out by Easter and then out by Fourth of July and out by Thanksgiving, and then it was Christmas again.' Then Stockdale turned to me and said, 'You know, I think they all died of broken hearts.'"

In the business world, Collins found the same unblinking attitude shared by executives at all the most successful companies he studied.

Like Stockdale, resilient people have very sober and down-to-earth views of those parts of reality that matter for survival. That's not to say that optimism doesn't have its place: In turning around a demoralized sales force, for instance, conjuring a sense of possibility can be a very powerful tool. But for bigger challenges, a cool, almost pessimistic, sense of reality is far more important.

Perhaps you're asking yourself, "Do I truly understand—and accept—the reality of my situation? Does my organization?" Those are good questions, particularly because research suggests most people slip into denial as a coping mechanism. Facing reality, really facing it, is grueling work. Indeed, it can be unpleasant and often emotionally wrenching. Consider the following story of organizational resilience, and see what it means to confront reality.

Prior to September 11, 2001, Morgan Stanley, the famous investment bank, was the largest tenant in the World Trade Center. The company had some 2,700 employees working in the south tower on 22 floors between the 43rd and the 74th. On that horrible day, the first plane hit the north tower at 8:46 AM, and Morgan Stanley started evacuating just one minute later, at 8:47 AM. When the second plane crashed into the south tower 15 minutes after that, Morgan Stanley's offices were largely empty. All told, the company lost only seven employees despite receiving an almost direct hit.

Of course, the organization was just plain lucky to be in the second tower. Cantor Fitzgerald, whose offices were hit in the first attack, couldn't have done anything to save its employees. Still, it was Morgan Stanley's hard-nosed realism that enabled the company to benefit from its luck. Soon after the 1993 attack on the World Trade Center, senior management recognized that working in such a symbolic center of U.S. commercial power made the company vulnerable to attention from terrorists and possible attack.

With this grim realization, Morgan Stanley launched a program of preparedness at the micro level. Few companies take their fire drills seriously. Not so Morgan Stanley, whose VP of security for the Individual Investor Group, Rick Rescorla, brought a military discipline to the job. Rescorla, himself a highly resilient, decorated Vietnam vet, made sure that people were fully drilled about what to do in a catastrophe. When disaster struck on September 11, Rescorla was on a bullhorn telling Morgan Stanley employees to stay calm and follow their well-practiced drill, even though some building supervisors were telling occupants that all was well. Sadly, Rescorla himself, whose life story has been widely covered in recent months, was one of the seven who didn't make it out.

"When you're in financial services where so much depends on technology, contingency planning is a major part of your business," says President and COO Robert G. Scott. But Morgan Stanley was prepared for the very toughest reality. It had not just one, but three, recovery sites where employees could congregate and business could take place if work locales were ever disrupted. "Multiple backup sites seemed like an incredible extravagance on September 10," concedes Scott. "But on September 12, they seemed like genius."

Maybe it was genius; it was undoubtedly resilience at work. The fact is, when we truly stare down reality, we prepare ourselves to act in ways that allow us to endure and survive extraordinary hardship. We train ourselves how to survive before the fact.

The Search for Meaning

The ability to see reality is closely linked to the second building block of resilience, the propensity to make meaning of terrible times. We all know people who, under duress, throw up their hands and cry, "How can this be happening to me?" Such people see themselves as victims, and living through hardship carries no lessons for them. But resilient people devise constructs about their suffering to create some sort of meaning for themselves and others.

I have a friend I'll call Jackie Oiseaux who suffered repeated psychoses over a ten-year period due to an undiagnosed bipolar disorder. Today, she holds down a big job in one of the top publishing companies in the country, has a family, and is a prominent member of her church community. When people ask her how she bounced back from her crises, she runs her hands through her hair. "People sometimes say, 'Why me?' But I've always said, 'Why *not* me?' True, I lost many things during my illness," she says, "but I found many more—incredible friends who saw me through the bleakest times and who will give meaning to my life forever."

This dynamic of meaning making is, most researchers agree, the way resilient people build bridges from present-day hardships to a fuller, better constructed future. Those bridges make the present manageable, for lack of a better word, removing the sense that the present is overwhelming. This concept was beautifully articulated by Viktor E. Frankl, an Austrian psychiatrist and an Auschwitz survivor. In the midst of staggering suffering, Frankl invented "meaning therapy," a humanistic therapy technique that helps individuals make the kinds of decisions that will create significance in their lives.

In his book *Man's Search for Meaning*, Frankl described the pivotal moment in the camp when he developed meaning therapy. He was on his way to work one day, worrying whether he should trade his last cigarette for a bowl of soup. He wondered how he was going to work with a new foreman whom he knew to be particularly sadistic. Suddenly, he was disgusted by just how trivial and meaningless his life had become. He realized that to survive, he had to find some purpose. Frankl did so by imagining himself giving a lecture after the war on the psychology of the concentration camp, to help outsiders understand what he had been through. Although he wasn't even sure he would survive, Frankl created some concrete goals for himself. In doing so, he succeeded in rising above the sufferings of the moment. As he put it in his book: "We must never forget that we may also find meaning in life even when confronted with a hopeless situation, when facing a fate that cannot be changed."

Frankl's theory underlies most resilience coaching in business. Indeed, I was struck by how often businesspeople referred to his work. "Resilience training—what we call hardiness—is a way for us to help people construct meaning in their everyday lives," explains Salvatore R. Maddi, a University of California, Irvine psychology professor and the director of the Hardiness Institute in Newport Beach, California. "When people realize the power of resilience training, they often say, 'Doc, is this what psychotherapy is?' But psychotherapy is for people whose lives have fallen apart badly and need repair. We see our work as showing people life skills and attitudes. Maybe those things should be taught at home, maybe they should be taught in schools, but they're not. So we end up doing it in business."

Yet the challenge confronting resilience trainers is often more difficult than we might imagine. Meaning can be elusive, and just because you found it once doesn't mean you'll keep it or find it again. Consider Aleksandr Solzhenitsyn, who survived the war against the Nazis, imprisonment in the gulag, and cancer. Yet when he moved to a farm in peaceful, safe Vermont, he could not cope with the "infantile West." He was unable to discern any real meaning in what he felt to be the destructive and irresponsible freedom of the West. Upset by his critics, he withdrew into his farmhouse, behind a locked fence, seldom to be seen in public. In 1994, a bitter man, Solzhenitsyn moved back to Russia.

Since finding meaning in one's environment is such an important aspect of resilience, it should come as no surprise that the most successful organizations and people possess strong value systems. Strong values infuse an environment with meaning because they offer ways to interpret and shape events. While it's popular these days to ridicule values, it's surely no coincidence that the most resilient organization in the world has been the Catholic Church, which has survived wars, corruption, and schism for more than 2,000 years, thanks largely to its immutable set of values. Businesses that survive also have their creeds, which give them purposes beyond just making money. Strikingly, many companies describe their value systems in religious terms. Pharmaceutical giant Johnson & Johnson, for instance, calls its value system, set out in a document given to every new employee at orientation, the Credo. Parcel company UPS talks constantly about its Noble Purpose.

Value systems at resilient companies change very little over the years and are used as scaffolding in times of trouble. UPS Chairman and CEO Mike Eskew believes that the Noble Purpose helped the company to rally after the agonizing strike in 1997. Says Eskew: "It was a hugely difficult time, like a family feud. Everyone had close friends on both sides of the fence, and it was tough for us to pick sides. But what saved us was our Noble Purpose. Whatever side people were on, they all shared a common set of values. Those values are core to us and never change; they frame most of our important decisions. Our strategy and our mission may change, but our values never do."

The religious connotations of words like "credo," "values," and "noble purpose," however, should not be confused with the actual content of the values. Companies can hold ethically questionable values and still be very resilient. Consider Phillip Morris, which has demonstrated impressive resilience in the face of increasing unpopularity. As Jim Collins points out, Phillip Morris has very strong values, although we might not agree with them—for instance, the value of "adult choice." But there's no doubt that Phillip Morris executives believe strongly in its values, and the strength of their beliefs sets the company apart from most of the other tobacco companies. In this context, it is worth noting that resilience is neither ethically good nor bad. It is merely the skill and the capacity to be robust under conditions of enormous stress and change. As Viktor Frankl wrote: "On the average, only those prisoners could keep alive who, after years of trekking from camp to camp, had lost all scruples in their fight for existence; they were prepared to use every means, honest and otherwise, even brutal..., in order to save themselves. We who have come back ... we know: The best of us did not return."

Values, positive or negative, are actually more important for organizational resilience than having resilient people on the payroll. If resilient employees are all interpreting reality in different ways, their decisions and actions may well conflict, calling into doubt the survival of their organization. And as the weakness of an organization becomes apparent, highly resilient individuals are more likely to jettison the organization than to imperil their own survival.

Ritualized Ingenuity

The third building block of resilience is the ability to make do with whatever is at hand. Psychologists follow the lead of French anthropologist Claude Levi-Strauss in calling this skill bricolage.[1] Intriguingly, the roots of that word are closely tied to the concept of resilience, which literally means "bouncing back." Says Levi-Strauss: "In its old sense, the verb *bricoler* ... was always used with reference to some extraneous movement: a ball rebounding, a dog straying, or a horse swerving from its direct course to avoid an obstacle."

Bricolage in the modern sense can be defined as a kind of inventiveness, an ability to improvise a solution to a problem without proper or obvious tools or materials. *Bricoleurs* are always tinkering—building radios from household effects or fixing their own cars. They make the most of what they have, putting objects to unfamiliar uses. In the concentration camps, for example, resilient inmates knew to pocket pieces of string or wire whenever they found them. The string or wire might later become useful—to fix a pair of shoes, perhaps, which in freezing conditions might make the difference between life and death.

When situations unravel, bricoleurs muddle through, imagining possibilities where others are confounded. I have two friends, whom I'll call Paul Shields and Mike Andrews, who were roommates throughout their college years. To no one's surprise, when they graduated, they set up a business together, selling educational materials to schools, businesses, and consulting firms. At first, the company was a great success, making both founders paper millionaires. But the recession of the early 1990s hit the company hard, and many core clients fell away. At the same time, Paul experienced a bitter divorce and a depression that made it impossible for him to work. Mike offered to buy Paul out but was instead slapped with a lawsuit claiming that Mike was trying to steal the business. At this point, a less resilient person might have just walked away from the mess. Not Mike. As the case wound through the courts, he kept the company going any way he could—constantly morphing the business until he found a model that worked: going into joint ventures to sell English-language training materials to Russian and Chinese companies. Later, he branched off into publishing newsletters for clients. At one point, he was even writing video scripts for his competitors. Thanks to all this bricolage, by the time the lawsuit was settled in his favor, Mike had an entirely different, and much more solid, business than the one he had started with.

Bricolage can be practiced on a higher level as well. Richard Feynman, winner of the 1965 Nobel Prize in physics, exemplified what I like to think of as intellectual bricolage. Out of pure curiosity,

Feynman made himself an expert on cracking safes, not only looking at the mechanics of safecracking but also cobbling together psychological insights about people who used safes and set the locks. He cracked many of the safes at Los Alamos, for instance, because he guessed that theoretical physicists would not set the locks with random code numbers they might forget but would instead use a sequence with mathematical significance. It turned out that the three safes containing all the secrets to the atomic bomb were set to the same mathematical constant, *e,* whose first six digits are 2.71828.

Resilient organizations are stuffed with bricoleurs, though not all of them, of course, are Richard Feynmans. Indeed, companies that survive regard improvisation as a core skill. Consider UPS, which empowers its drivers to do whatever it takes to deliver packages on time. Says CEO Eskew: "We tell our employees to get the job done. If that means they need to improvise, they improvise. Otherwise we just couldn't do what we do every day. Just think what can go wrong: a busted traffic light, a flat tire, a bridge washed out. If a snowstorm hits Louisville tonight, a group of people will sit together and discuss how to handle the problem. Nobody tells them to do that. They come together because it's our tradition to do so."

That tradition meant that the company was delivering parcels in southeast Florida just one day after Hurricane Andrew devastated the region in 1992, causing billions of dollars in damage. Many people were living in their cars because their homes had been destroyed, yet UPS drivers and managers sorted packages at a diversion site and made deliveries even to those who were stranded in their cars. It was largely UPS's improvisational skills that enabled it to keep functioning after the catastrophic hit. And the fact that the company continued on gave others a sense of purpose or meaning amid the chaos.

Improvisation of the sort practiced by UPS, however, is a far cry from unbridled creativity. Indeed, much like the military, UPS lives on rules and regulations. As Eskew says: "Drivers always put their keys in the same place. They close the doors the same way. They wear their uniforms the same way. We are a company of precision." He believes that although they may seem stifling, UPS's rules were what allowed the company to bounce back immediately after Hurricane

Andrew, for they enabled people to focus on the one or two fixes they needed to make in order to keep going.

Eskew's opinion is echoed by Karl E. Weick, a professor of organizational behavior at the University of Michigan Business School in Ann Arbor and one of the most respected thinkers on organizational psychology. "There is good evidence that when people are put under pressure, they regress to their most habituated ways of responding," Weick has written. "What we do not expect under life-threatening pressure is creativity." In other words, the rules and regulations that make some companies appear less creative may actually make them more resilient in times of real turbulence.

Claus Schmidt, the newsman I mentioned earlier, died about five years ago, but I'm not sure I could have interviewed him about his own resilience even if he were alive. It would have felt strange, I think, to ask him, "Claus, did you really face down reality? Did you make meaning out of your hardships? Did you improvise your recovery after each professional and personal disaster?" He may not have been able to answer. In my experience, resilient people don't often describe themselves that way. They shrug off their survival stories and very often assign them to luck.

Obviously, luck does have a lot to do with surviving. It was luck that Morgan Stanley was situated in the south tower and could put its preparedness training to work. But being lucky is not the same as being resilient. Resilience is a reflex, a way of facing and understanding the world, that is deeply etched into a person's mind and soul. Resilient people and companies face reality with staunchness, make meaning of hardship instead of crying out in despair, and improvise solutions from thin air. Others do not. This is the nature of resilience, and we will never completely understand it.

Originally published in May 2002. Reprint R0205B

Note

1. See, e.g., Karl E. Weick, "The Collapse of Sense-making in Organizations: The Mann Gulch Disaster," *Administrative Science Quarterly*, December 1993.

Manage Your Energy, Not Your Time

by Tony Schwartz and Catherine McCarthy

STEVE WANNER IS A HIGHLY respected 37-year-old partner at Ernst & Young, married with four young children. When we met him a year ago, he was working 12- to 14-hour days, felt perpetually exhausted, and found it difficult to fully engage with his family in the evenings, which left him feeling guilty and dissatisfied. He slept poorly, made no time to exercise, and seldom ate healthy meals, instead grabbing a bite to eat on the run or while working at his desk.

Wanner's experience is not uncommon. Most of us respond to rising demands in the workplace by putting in longer hours, which inevitably take a toll on us physically, mentally, and emotionally. That leads to declining levels of engagement, increasing levels of distraction, high turnover rates, and soaring medical costs among employees. We at the Energy Project have worked with thousands of leaders and managers in the course of doing consulting and coaching at large organizations during the past five years. With remarkable consistency, these executives tell us they're pushing themselves harder than ever to keep up and increasingly feel they are at a breaking point.

The core problem with working longer hours is that time is a finite resource. Energy is a different story. Defined in physics as the capacity to work, energy comes from four main wellsprings in human beings: the body, emotions, mind, and spirit. In each, energy can be systematically expanded and regularly renewed by establishing specific rituals—behaviors that are intentionally practiced and precisely scheduled, with the goal of making them unconscious and automatic as quickly as possible.

To effectively reenergize their workforces, organizations need to shift their emphasis from getting more out of people to investing more in them, so they are motivated—and able—to bring more of themselves to work every day. To recharge themselves, individuals need to recognize the costs of energy-depleting behaviors and then take responsibility for changing them, regardless of the circumstances they're facing.

The rituals and behaviors Wanner established to better manage his energy transformed his life. He set an earlier bedtime and gave up drinking, which had disrupted his sleep. As a consequence, when he woke up he felt more rested and more motivated to exercise, which he now does almost every morning. In less than two months he lost 15 pounds. After working out he now sits down with his family for breakfast. Wanner still puts in long hours on the job, but he renews himself regularly along the way. He leaves his desk for lunch and usually takes a morning and an afternoon walk outside. When he arrives at home in the evening, he's more relaxed and better able to connect with his wife and children.

Establishing simple rituals like these can lead to striking results across organizations. At Wachovia Bank, we took a group of employees through a pilot energy management program and then measured their performance against that of a control group. The participants outperformed the controls on a series of financial metrics, such as the value of loans they generated. They also reported substantial improvements in their customer relationships, their engagement with work, and their personal satisfaction. In this article, we'll describe the Wachovia study in a little more detail. Then we'll explain what executives and managers can do to increase and regularly renew work capacity—the approach used by the Energy Project, which builds on, deepens, and extends several core concepts developed by Tony's former partner Jim Loehr in his seminal work with athletes.

Idea in Brief

Organizations are demanding ever-higher performance from their workforces. People are trying to comply, but the usual method—putting in longer hours—has backfired. They're getting exhausted, disengaged, and sick. And they're defecting to healthier job environments.

Longer days at the office don't work because time is a limited resource. But personal energy is renewable, say Schwartz and McCarthy. By fostering deceptively simple **rituals** that help employees regularly replenish their energy, organizations build workers' physical, emotional, and mental resilience. These rituals include taking brief breaks at specific intervals, expressing appreciation to others, reducing interruptions, and spending more time on activities people do best and enjoy most.

Help your employees systematically rejuvenate their personal energy, and the benefits go straight to your bottom line. Take Wachovia Bank: Participants in an energy renewal program produced 13 percentage points greater year-over-year in revenues from loans than a control group did. And they exceeded the control group's gains in revenues from deposits by 20 percentage points.

Linking Capacity and Performance at Wachovia

Most large organizations invest in developing employees' skills, knowledge, and competence. Very few help build and sustain their capacity—their energy—which is typically taken for granted. In fact, greater capacity makes it possible to get more done in less time at a higher level of engagement and with more sustainability. Our experience at Wachovia bore this out.

In early 2006 we took 106 employees at 12 regional banks in southern New Jersey through a curriculum of four modules, each of which focused on specific strategies for strengthening one of the four main dimensions of energy. We delivered it at one-month intervals to groups of approximately 20 to 25, ranging from senior leaders to lower-level managers. We also assigned each attendee a fellow employee as a source of support between sessions. Using Wachovia's own key performance metrics, we evaluated how the participant group performed compared with a group of employees at similar levels at a nearby set of Wachovia banks who did not go through the

Idea in Practice

Schwartz and McCarthy recommend these practices for renewing four dimensions of personal energy.

Physical Energy

- Enhance your sleep by setting an earlier bedtime and reducing alcohol use.

- Reduce stress by engaging in cardiovascular activity at least three times a week and strength training at least once.

- Eat small meals and light snacks every three hours.

- Learn to notice signs of imminent energy flagging, including restlessness, yawning, hunger, and difficulty concentrating.

- Take brief but regular breaks, away from your desk, at 90- to 120-minute intervals throughout the day.

Emotional Energy

- Defuse negative emotions—irritability, impatience, anxiety, insecurity—through deep abdominal breathing.

- Fuel positive emotions in yourself and others by regularly expressing appreciation to others in detailed, specific terms through notes, e-mails, calls, or conversations.

- Look at upsetting situations through new lenses. Adopt a "reverse lens" to ask, "What would the other person in this conflict say, and how might he be right?" Use a "long lens" to ask, "How will I likely view this situation in six months?" Employ a "wide lens" to ask, "How can I grow and learn from this situation?"

Mental Energy

- Reduce interruptions by performing high-concentration tasks away from phones and e-mail.

- Respond to voice mails and e-mails at designated times during the day.

training. To create a credible basis for comparison, we looked at year-over-year percentage changes in performance across several metrics.

On a measure called the "Big 3"—revenues from three kinds of loans—the participants showed a year-over-year increase that was 13 percentage points greater than the control group's in the first three months of our study. On revenues from deposits, the participants exceeded the control group's year-over-year gain by 20 percentage points during that same period. The precise gains varied month by month, but with only a handful of exceptions, the participants

- Every night, identify the most important challenge for the next day. Then make it your first priority when you arrive at work in the morning.

Spiritual Energy

- Identify your "sweet spot" activities—those that give you feelings of effectiveness, effortless absorption, and fulfillment. Find ways to do more of these. One executive who hated doing sales reports delegated them to someone who loved that activity.

- Allocate time and energy to what you consider most important. For example, spend the last 20 minutes of your evening commute relaxing, so you can connect with your family once you're home.

- Live your core values. For instance, if consideration is important to you but you're perpetually late for meetings, practice intentionally showing up five minutes early for meetings.

How Companies Can Help

To support energy renewal rituals in your firm:

- Build "renewal rooms" where people can go to relax and re-fuel.

- Subsidize gym memberships.

- Encourage managers to gather employees for midday workouts.

- Suggest that people stop checking e-mails during meetings.

continued to significantly outperform the control group for a full year after completing the program. Although other variables undoubtedly influenced these outcomes, the participants' superior performance was notable in its consistency. (See the exhibit "How Energy Renewal Programs Boosted Productivity at Wachovia.")

We also asked participants how the program influenced them personally. Sixty-eight percent reported that it had a positive impact on their relationships with clients and customers. Seventy-one percent said that it had a noticeable or substantial positive impact on their

---

How energy renewal programs boosted productivity at Wachovia

At Wachovia Bank, employees participating in an energy renewal program outperformed a control group of employees, demonstrating significantly greater improvements in year-over-year performance during the first quarter of 2006.

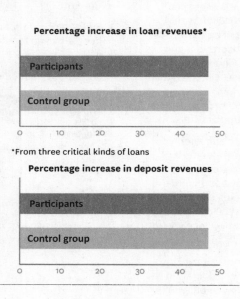

Percentage increase in loan revenues*

Participants

Control group

0   10   20   30   40   50

*From three critical kinds of loans

Percentage increase in deposit revenues

Participants

Control group

0   10   20   30   40   50

---

productivity and performance. These findings corroborated a raft of anecdotal evidence we've gathered about the effectiveness of this approach among leaders at other large companies such as Ernst & Young, Sony, Deutsche Bank, Nokia, ING Direct, Ford, and MasterCard.

The Body: Physical Energy

Our program begins by focusing on physical energy. It is scarcely news that inadequate nutrition, exercise, sleep, and rest diminish people's basic energy levels, as well as their ability to manage their emotions and focus their attention. Nonetheless, many executives don't find ways to practice consistently healthy behaviors, given all the other demands in their lives.

Before participants in our program begin to explore ways to increase their physical energy, they take an energy audit, which includes four questions in each energy dimension—body, emotions, mind, and spirit. (See the exhibit "Are You Headed for an Energy Crisis?") On average, participants get eight to ten of those 16 questions "wrong," meaning they're doing things such as skipping breakfast, failing to express appreciation to others, struggling to focus on one thing at a time, or spending too little time on activities that give them a sense of purpose. While most participants aren't surprised to learn these behaviors are counterproductive, having them all listed in one place is often uncomfortable, sobering, and galvanizing. The audit highlights employees' greatest energy deficits. Participants also fill out charts designed to raise their awareness about how their exercise, diet, and sleep practices influence their energy levels.

The next step is to identify rituals for building and renewing physical energy. When Gary Faro, a vice president at Wachovia, began the program, he was significantly overweight, ate poorly, lacked a regular exercise routine, worked long hours, and typically slept no more than five or six hours a night. That is not an unusual profile among the leaders and managers we see. Over the course of the program, Faro began regular cardiovascular and strength training. He started going to bed at a designated time and sleeping longer. He changed his eating habits from two big meals a day ("Where I usually gorged myself," he says) to smaller meals and light snacks every three hours. The aim was to help him stabilize his glucose levels over the course of the day, avoiding peaks and valleys. He lost 50 pounds in the process, and his energy levels soared. "I used to schedule tough projects for the morning, when I knew that I would be more focused," Faro says. "I don't have to do that anymore because I find that I'm just as focused now at 5 PM as I am at 8 AM."

Another key ritual Faro adopted was to take brief but regular breaks at specific intervals throughout the workday—always leaving his desk. The value of such breaks is grounded in our physiology.

Are you headed for an energy crisis?

Please check the statements below that are true for you.

Body

☐ I don't regularly get at least seven to eight hours of sleep, and I often wake up feeling tired.

☐ I frequently skip breakfast, or I settle for something that isn't nutritious.

☐ I don't work out enough (meaning cardiovascular training at least three times a week and strength training at least once a week).

☐ I don't take regular breaks during the day to truly renew and recharge, or I often eat lunch at my desk, if I eat it at all.

Emotions

☐ I frequently find myself feeling irritable, impatient, or anxious at work, especially when work is demanding.

☐ I don't have enough time with my family and loved ones, and when I'm with them, I'm not always really with them.

☐ I have too little time for the activities that I most deeply enjoy.

☐ I don't stop frequently enough to express my appreciation to others or to savor my accomplishments and blessings.

Mind

☐ I have difficulty focusing on one thing at a time, and I am easily distracted during the day, especially by e-mail.

☐ I spend much of my day reacting to immediate crises and demands rather than focusing on activities with longer-term value and high leverage.

☐ I don't take enough time for reflection, strategizing, and creative thinking.

☐ I work in the evenings or on weekends, and I almost never take an e-mail–free vacation.

Spirit

☐ I don't spend enough time at work doing what I do best and enjoy most.

☐ There are significant gaps between what I say is most important to me in my life and how I actually allocate my time and energy.

☐ My decisions at work are more often influenced by external demands than by a strong, clear sense of my own purpose.

☐ I don't invest enough time and energy in making a positive difference to others or to the world.

How is your overall energy?

Total number of statements checked: __

Guide to scores

0–3: Excellent energy management skills
4–6: Reasonable energy management skills

(continued)

7–10: Significant energy management deficits
11–16: A full-fledged energy management crisis

What do you need to work on?

Number of checks in each category:
Body __
Mind __
Emotions __
Spirit __

Guide to category scores

0: Excellent energy management skills
1: Strong energy management skills
2: Significant deficits
3: Poor energy management skills
4: A full-fledged energy crisis

"Ultradian rhythms" refer to 90- to 120-minute cycles during which our bodies slowly move from a high-energy state into a physiological trough. Toward the end of each cycle, the body begins to crave a period of recovery. The signals include physical restlessness, yawning, hunger, and difficulty concentrating, but many of us ignore them and keep working. The consequence is that our energy reservoir—our remaining capacity—burns down as the day wears on.

Intermittent breaks for renewal, we have found, result in higher and more sustainable performance. The length of renewal is less important than the quality. It is possible to get a great deal of recovery in a short time—as little as several minutes—if it involves a ritual that allows you to disengage from work and truly change channels. That could range from getting up to talk to a colleague about something other than work, to listening to music on an iPod, to walking up and down stairs in an office building. While breaks are countercultural in most organizations and counterintuitive for many high achievers, their value is multifaceted.

Matthew Lang is a managing director for Sony in South Africa. He adopted some of the same rituals that Faro did, including a

20-minute walk in the afternoons. Lang's walk not only gives him a mental and emotional breather and some exercise but also has become the time when he gets his best creative ideas. That's because when he walks he is not actively thinking, which allows the dominant left hemisphere of his brain to give way to the right hemisphere with its greater capacity to see the big picture and make imaginative leaps.

The Emotions: Quality of Energy

When people are able to take more control of their emotions, they can improve the quality of their energy, regardless of the external pressures they're facing. To do this, they first must become more aware of how they feel at various points during the workday and of the impact these emotions have on their effectiveness. Most people realize that they tend to perform best when they're feeling positive energy. What they find surprising is that they're not able to perform well or to lead effectively when they're feeling any other way.

Unfortunately, without intermittent recovery, we're not physiologically capable of sustaining highly positive emotions for long periods. Confronted with relentless demands and unexpected challenges, people tend to slip into negative emotions—the fight-or-flight mode—often multiple times in a day. They become irritable and impatient, or anxious and insecure. Such states of mind drain people's energy and cause friction in their relationships. Fight-or-flight emotions also make it impossible to think clearly, logically, and reflectively. When executives learn to recognize what kinds of events trigger their negative emotions, they gain greater capacity to take control of their reactions.

One simple but powerful ritual for defusing negative emotions is what we call "buying time." Deep abdominal breathing is one way to do that. Exhaling slowly for five or six seconds induces relaxation and recovery, and turns off the fight-or-flight response. When we began working with Fujio Nishida, president of Sony Europe, he had a habit of lighting up a cigarette each time something especially stressful occurred—at least two or three times a day. Otherwise, he didn't smoke. We taught him the breathing exercise as an alternative, and it worked immediately: Nishida found he no longer had the desire for a cigarette. It wasn't the smoking that had given him relief from the stress, we concluded, but the relaxation prompted by the deep inhalation and exhalation.

A powerful ritual that fuels positive emotions is expressing appreciation to others, a practice that seems to be as beneficial to the giver as to the receiver. It can take the form of a handwritten note, an e-mail, a call, or a conversation—and the more detailed and specific, the higher the impact. As with all rituals, setting aside a particular time to do it vastly increases the chances of success. Ben Jenkins, vice chairman and president of the General Bank at Wachovia in Charlotte, North Carolina, built his appreciation ritual into time set aside for mentoring. He began scheduling lunches or dinners regularly with people who worked for him. Previously, the only sit-downs he'd had with his direct reports were to hear monthly reports on their numbers or to give them yearly performance reviews. Now, over meals, he makes it a priority to recognize their accomplishments and also to talk with them about their lives and their aspirations rather than their immediate work responsibilities.

Finally, people can cultivate positive emotions by learning to change the stories they tell themselves about the events in their lives. Often, people in conflict cast themselves in the role of victim, blaming others or external circumstances for their problems. Becoming aware of the difference between the facts in a given situation and the way we interpret those facts can be powerful in itself. It's been a revelation for many of the people we work with to discover they have a choice about how to view a given event and to recognize how powerfully the story they tell influences the emotions they feel. We teach them to tell the most hopeful and personally empowering story possible in any given situation, without denying or minimizing the facts.

The most effective way people can change a story is to view it through any of three new lenses, which are all alternatives to seeing the world from the victim perspective. With the *reverse lens*, for example, people ask themselves, "What would the other person in this conflict say and in what ways might that be true?" With the *long lens* they ask, "How will I most likely view this situation in six months?"

With the *wide lens* they ask themselves, "Regardless of the outcome of this issue, how can I grow and learn from it?" Each of these lenses can help people intentionally cultivate more positive emotions.

Nicolas Babin, director of corporate communications for Sony Europe, was the point person for calls from reporters when Sony went through several recalls of its batteries in 2006. Over time he found his work increasingly exhausting and dispiriting. After practicing the lens exercises, he began finding ways to tell himself a more positive and empowering story about his role. "I realized," he explains, "that this was an opportunity for me to build stronger relationships with journalists by being accessible to them and to increase Sony's credibility by being straightforward and honest."

The Mind: Focus of Energy

Many executives view multitasking as a necessity in the face of all the demands they juggle, but it actually undermines productivity. Distractions are costly: A temporary shift in attention from one task to another—stopping to answer an e-mail or take a phone call, for instance—increases the amount of time necessary to finish the primary task by as much as 25%, a phenomenon known as "switching time." It's far more efficient to fully focus for 90 to 120 minutes, take a true break, and then fully focus on the next activity. We refer to these work periods as "ultradian sprints."

Once people see how much they struggle to concentrate, they can create rituals to reduce the relentless interruptions that technology has introduced in their lives. We start out with an exercise that forces them to face the impact of daily distractions. They attempt to complete a complex task and are regularly interrupted—an experience that, people report, ends up feeling much like everyday life.

Dan Cluna, a vice president at Wachovia, designed two rituals to better focus his attention. The first one is to leave his desk and go into a conference room, away from phones and e-mail, whenever he has a task that requires concentration. He now finishes reports in a third of the time they used to require. Cluna built his second ritual around meetings at branches with the financial specialists who report to him. Previously, he would answer his phone whenever it rang during these meetings. As a consequence, the meetings he scheduled for an hour often stretched to two, and he rarely gave anyone his full attention. Now Cluna lets his phone go to voice mail, so that he can focus completely on the person in front of him. He now answers the accumulated voice-mail messages when he has downtime between meetings.

E&Y's hard-charging Wanner used to answer e-mail constantly throughout the day—whenever he heard a "ping." Then he created a ritual of checking his e-mail just twice a day—at 10:15 AM and 2:30 PM. Whereas previously he couldn't keep up with all his messages, he discovered he could clear his in-box each time he opened it— the reward of fully focusing his attention on e-mail for 45 minutes at a time. Wanner has also reset the expectations of all the people he regularly communicates with by e-mail. "I've told them if it's an emergency and they need an instant response, they can call me and I'll always pick up," he says. Nine months later he has yet to receive such a call.

Michael Henke, a senior manager at E&Y, sat his team down at the start of the busy season last winter and told them that at certain points during the day he was going to turn off his Sametime (an in-house instant-message system). The result, he said, was that he would be less available to them for questions. Like Wanner, he told his team to call him if any emergency arose, but they rarely did. He also encouraged the group to take regular breaks throughout the day and to eat more regularly. They finished the busy season under budget and more profitable than other teams that hadn't followed the energy renewal program. "We got the same amount of work done in less time," says Henke. "It made for a win-win."

Another way to mobilize mental energy is to focus systematically on activities that have the most long-term leverage. Unless people intentionally schedule time for more challenging work, they tend not to get to it at all or rush through it at the last minute. Perhaps the most effective focus ritual the executives we work with have adopted is to identify each night the most important challenge for the next day and make it their very first priority when they arrive in the morning. Jean Luc Duquesne, a vice president for Sony Europe in

Paris, used to answer his e-mail as soon as he got to the office, just as many people do. He now tries to concentrate the first hour of every day on the most important topic. He finds that he often emerges at 10 AM feeling as if he's already had a productive day.

The Human Spirit: Energy of Meaning and Purpose

People tap into the energy of the human spirit when their everyday work and activities are consistent with what they value most and with what gives them a sense of meaning and purpose. If the work they're doing really matters to them, they typically feel more positive energy, focus better, and demonstrate greater perseverance. Regrettably, the high demands and fast pace of corporate life don't leave much time to pay attention to these issues, and many people don't even recognize meaning and purpose as potential sources of energy. Indeed, if we tried to begin our program by focusing on the human spirit, it would likely have minimal impact. Only when participants have experienced the value of the rituals they establish in the other dimensions do they start to see that being attentive to their own deeper needs dramatically influences their effectiveness and satisfaction at work.

For E&Y partner Jonathan Anspacher, simply having the opportunity to ask himself a series of questions about what really mattered to him was both illuminating and energizing. "I think it's important to be a little introspective and say, 'What do you want to be remembered for?'" he told us. "You don't want to be remembered as the crazy partner who worked these long hours and had his people be miserable. When my kids call me and ask, 'Can you come to my band concert?' I want to say, 'Yes, I'll be there and I'll be in the front row.' I don't want to be the father that comes in and sits in the back and is on his Blackberry and has to step out to take a phone call."

To access the energy of the human spirit, people need to clarify priorities and establish accompanying rituals in three categories: doing what they do best and enjoy most at work; consciously allocating time and energy to the areas of their lives—work, family, health, service to others—they deem most important; and living their core values in their daily behaviors.

When you're attempting to discover what you do best and what you enjoy most, it's important to realize that these two things aren't necessarily mutually inclusive. You may get lots of positive feedback about something you're very good at but not truly enjoy it. Conversely, you can love doing something but have no gift for it, so that achieving success requires much more energy than it makes sense to invest.

To help program participants discover their areas of strength, we ask them to recall at least two work experiences in the past several months during which they found themselves in their "sweet spot"— feeling effective, effortlessly absorbed, inspired, and fulfilled. Then we have them deconstruct those experiences to understand precisely what energized them so positively and what specific talents they were drawing on. If leading strategy feels like a sweet spot, for example, is it being in charge that's most invigorating or participating in a creative endeavor? Or is it using a skill that comes to you easily and so feels good to exercise? Finally, we have people establish a ritual that will encourage them to do more of exactly that kind of activity at work.

A senior leader we worked with realized that one of the activities he least liked was reading and summarizing detailed sales reports, whereas one of his favorites was brainstorming new strategies. The leader found a direct report who loved immersing himself in numbers and delegated the sales report task to him—happily settling for brief oral summaries from him each day. The leader also began scheduling a free-form 90-minute strategy session every other week with the most creative people in his group.

In the second category, devoting time and energy to what's important to you, there is often a similar divide between what people say is important and what they actually do. Rituals can help close this gap. When Jean Luc Duquesne, the Sony Europe vice president, thought hard about his personal priorities, he realized that spending time with his family was what mattered most to him, but it often got squeezed out of his day. So he instituted a ritual in which he switches off for at least three hours every evening when he gets home, so he can focus on his family. "I'm still not an expert on

PlayStation," he told us, "but according to my youngest son, I'm learning and I'm a good student." Steve Wanner, who used to talk on the cell phone all the way to his front door on his commute home, has chosen a specific spot 20 minutes from his house where he ends whatever call he's on and puts away the phone. He spends the rest of his commute relaxing so that when he does arrive home, he's less preoccupied with work and more available to his wife and children.

The third category, practicing your core values in your everyday behavior, is a challenge for many as well. Most people are living at such a furious pace that they rarely stop to ask themselves what they stand for and who they want to be. As a consequence, they let external demands dictate their actions.

We don't suggest that people explicitly define their values, because the results are usually too predictable. Instead, we seek to uncover them, in part by asking questions that are inadvertently revealing, such as, "What are the qualities that you find most off-putting when you see them in others?" By describing what they can't stand, people unintentionally divulge what they stand for. If you are very offended by stinginess, for example, generosity is probably one of your key values. If you are especially put off by rudeness in others, it's likely that consideration is a high value for you. As in the other categories, establishing rituals can help bridge the gap between the values you aspire to and how you currently behave. If you discover that consideration is a key value, but you are perpetually late for meetings, the ritual might be to end the meetings you run five minutes earlier than usual and intentionally show up five minutes early for the meeting that follows.

Addressing these three categories helps people go a long way toward achieving a greater sense of alignment, satisfaction, and well-being in their lives on and off the job. Those feelings are a source of positive energy in their own right and reinforce people's desire to persist at rituals in other energy dimensions as well.

This new way of working takes hold only to the degree that organizations support their people in adopting new behaviors. We have learned, sometimes painfully, that not all executives and companies are prepared to embrace the notion that personal renewal for employees will lead to better and more sustainable performance. To succeed, renewal efforts need solid support and commitment from senior management, beginning with the key decision maker.

At Wachovia, Susanne Svizeny, the president of the region in which we conducted our study, was the primary cheerleader for the program. She embraced the principles in her own life and made a series of personal changes, including a visible commitment to building more regular renewal rituals into her work life. Next, she took it upon herself to foster the excitement and commitment of her leadership team. Finally, she regularly reached out by e-mail to all participants in the project to encourage them in their rituals and seek their feedback. It was clear to everyone that she took the work seriously. Her enthusiasm was infectious, and the results spoke for themselves.

At Sony Europe, several hundred leaders have embraced the principles of energy management. Over the next year, more than 2,000 of their direct reports will go through the energy renewal program. From Fujio Nishida on down, it has become increasingly culturally acceptable at Sony to take intermittent breaks, work out at midday, answer e-mail only at designated times, and even ask colleagues who seem irritable or impatient what stories they're telling themselves.

Organizational support also entails shifts in policies, practices, and cultural messages. A number of firms we worked with have built "renewal rooms" where people can regularly go to relax and refuel. Others offer subsidized gym memberships. In some cases, leaders themselves gather groups of employees for midday workouts. One company instituted a no-meeting zone between 8 and 9 AM to ensure that people had at least one hour absolutely free of meetings. At several companies, including Sony, senior leaders collectively agreed to stop checking e-mail during meetings as a way to make the meetings more focused and efficient.

One factor that can get in the way of success is a crisis mentality. The optimal candidates for energy renewal programs are organizations that are feeling enough pain to be eager for new solutions but not so much that they're completely overwhelmed. At one organization where we had the active support of the CEO, the company was under intense pressure to grow rapidly, and the senior team couldn't tear themselves away from their focus on immediate survival—even though taking time out for renewal might have allowed them to be more productive at a more sustainable level.

By contrast, the group at Ernst & Young successfully went through the process at the height of tax season. With the permission of their leaders, they practiced defusing negative emotions by breathing or telling themselves different stories, and alternated highly focused periods of work with renewal breaks. Most people in the group reported that this busy season was the least stressful they'd ever experienced.

The implicit contract between organizations and their employees today is that each will try to get as much from the other as they can, as quickly as possible, and then move on without looking back. We believe that is mutually self-defeating. Both individuals and the organizations they work for end up depleted rather than enriched. Employees feel increasingly beleaguered and burned out. Organizations are forced to settle for employees who are less than fully engaged and to constantly hire and train new people to replace those who choose to leave. We envision a new and explicit contract that benefits all parties: Organizations invest in their people across all dimensions of their lives to help them build and sustain their value. Individuals respond by bringing all their multidimensional energy wholeheartedly to work every day. Both grow in value as a result.

Originally published in October 2007. Reprint R0710B

Overloaded Circuits

by Edward M. Hallowell

DAVID DRUMS HIS FINGERS on his desk as he scans the e-mail on his computer screen. At the same time, he's talking on the phone to an executive halfway around the world. His knee bounces up and down like a jackhammer. He intermittently bites his lip and reaches for his constant companion, the coffee cup. He's so deeply involved in multitasking that he has forgotten the appointment his Outlook calendar reminded him of 15 minutes ago.

Jane, a senior vice president, and Mike, her CEO, have adjoining offices so they can communicate quickly, yet communication never seems to happen. "Whenever I go into Mike's office, his phone lights up, my cell phone goes off, someone knocks on the door, he suddenly turns to his screen and writes an e-mail, or he tells me about a new issue he wants me to address," Jane complains. "We're working flat out just to stay afloat, and we're not getting anything important accomplished. It's driving me crazy."

David, Jane, and Mike aren't crazy, but they're certainly crazed. Their experience is becoming the norm for overworked managers who suffer—like many of your colleagues, and possibly like you—from a very real but unrecognized neurological phenomenon that I call attention deficit trait, or ADT. Caused by brain overload, ADT is now epidemic in organizations. The core symptoms are distractibility, inner frenzy, and impatience. People with ADT have difficulty staying organized, setting priorities, and managing time. These symptoms can undermine the work of an otherwise gifted executive. If

David, Jane, Mike, and the millions like them understood themselves in neurological terms, they could actively manage their lives instead of reacting to problems as they happen.

As a psychiatrist who has diagnosed and treated thousands of people over the past 25 years for a medical condition called attention deficit disorder, or ADD (now known clinically as attention-deficit/ hyperactivity disorder), I have observed firsthand how a rapidly growing segment of the adult population is developing this new, related condition. The number of people with ADT coming into my clinical practice has mushroomed by a factor of ten in the past decade. Unfortunately, most of the remedies for chronic overload proposed by time-management consultants and executive coaches do not address the underlying causes of ADT.

Unlike ADD, a neurological disorder that has a genetic component and can be aggravated by environmental and physical factors, ADT springs entirely from the environment. Like the traffic jam, ADT is an artifact of modern life. It is brought on by the demands on our time and attention that have exploded over the past two decades. As our minds fill with noise—feckless synaptic events signifying nothing—the brain gradually loses its capacity to attend fully and thoroughly to anything.

The symptoms of ADT come upon a person gradually. The sufferer doesn't experience a single crisis but rather a series of minor emergencies while he or she tries harder and harder to keep up. Shouldering a responsibility to "suck it up" and not complain as the workload increases, executives with ADT do whatever they can to handle a load they simply cannot manage as well as they'd like. The ADT sufferer therefore feels a constant low level of panic and guilt. Facing a tidal wave of tasks, the executive becomes increasingly hurried, curt, peremptory, and unfocused, while pretending that everything is fine.

To control ADT, we first have to recognize it. And control it we must, if we as individuals and organizational leaders are to be effective. In the following pages, I'll offer an analysis of the origins of ADT and provide some suggestions that may help you manage it.

Idea in Brief

Frenzied executives who fidget through meetings, miss appointments, and jab at the elevator's "door close" button aren't crazy— just crazed. They're suffering from a newly recognized neurological phenomenon called **attention deficit trait (ADT)**. Marked by distractibility, inner frenzy, and impatience, ADT prevents managers from clarifying priorities, making smart decisions, and managing their time. This insidious condition turns otherwise talented performers into harried underachievers. And it's reaching epidemic proportions.

ADT isn't an illness or character defect. It's our brains' natural response to exploding demands on our time and attention. As data increasingly floods our brains, we lose our ability to solve problems and handle the unknown. Creativity shrivels; mistakes multiply. Some sufferers eventually melt down.

How to control ADT's ravaging impact on performance? *Foster positive emotions* by connecting face-to-face with people you like throughout the day. *Take physical care of your brain* by getting enough sleep, eating healthfully, and exercising regularly. *Organize for ADT*, designating part of each day for thinking and planning, and setting up your office to foster mental functioning (for example, keeping part of your desk clear at all times).

These strategies may seem like no-brainers. But they'll help you vanquish the ADT demon before it can strike.

Attention Deficit Cousins

To understand the nature and treatment of ADT, it's useful to know something of its cousin, ADD.

Usually seen as a learning disability in children, ADD also afflicts about 5% of the adult population. Researchers using MRI scans have found that people with ADD suffer a slightly diminished volume in four specific brain regions that have various functions such as modulating emotion (especially anger and frustration) and assisting in learning. One of the regions, made up of the frontal and prefrontal lobes, generates thoughts, makes decisions, sets priorities, and organizes activities. While the medications used to treat ADD don't change

Idea in Practice

How You Can Combat ADT

Promote positive emotions.
Negative emotions—especially fear—can hamper productive brain functioning. To promote positive feelings, especially during highly stressful times, interact directly with someone you like at least every four to six hours. In environments where people are in physical contact with people they trust, brain functioning hums. By connecting comfortably with colleagues, you'll help your brain's "executive" center (responsible for decision making, planning, and information prioritizing) perform at its best.

Take physical care of your brain. Ample sleep, a good diet, and exercise are critical for staving off ADT. You're getting enough sleep if you can awake without an alarm clock. You're eating well if you're avoiding sugar and white flour and consuming more fruits, whole grains, vegetables, and protein instead. You're exercising enough if you're taking a brisk walk or going up and down a flight of stairs a few times a day.

Organize for ADT. Instead of getting sucked into the vortices of e-mail or voice mail first thing in the morning, attend to a critical task. With paperwork, apply the OHIO ("Only handle it once") rule: Whenever you touch a document,

act on it, file it, or throw it away. Do crucial work during times of the day when you perform at your best. Use whatever small strategies help you function well mentally—whether it's listening to music or walking around while working, or doodling during meetings. And before you leave for the day, list three to five priority items you'll need to address tomorrow.

What Your Company Can Do. In firms that ignore ADT symptoms, employees underachieve, create clutter, and cut corners. Careless mistakes, illness, and turnover increase, as people squander their brainpower. To counteract ADT and harness employees' brainpower, invest in amenities that foster a positive, productive atmosphere.

Example: Major software company SAS Institute creates a warm, connected, and relaxed work environment by offering employees perks such as a seven-hour workday that ends at 5:00; large on-site gym and day-care facility; and cafeteria that provides baby seats and high chairs so parents can eat lunch with their children. The payoff? Employees return the favors with high productivity. And SAS's turnover never exceeds 5%—saving the company millions on recruiting, training, and severance.

the anatomy of the brain, they alter brain chemistry, which in turn improves function in each of the four regions and so dramatically bolsters the performance of ADD sufferers.

ADD confers both disadvantages and advantages. The negative characteristics include a tendency to procrastinate and miss deadlines. People with ADD struggle with disorganization and tardiness; they can be forgetful and drift away mentally in the middle of a conversation or while reading. Their performance can be inconsistent: brilliant one moment and unsatisfactory the next. ADD sufferers also tend to demonstrate impatience and lose focus unless, oddly enough, they are under stress or handling multiple inputs. (This is because stress leads to the production of adrenaline, which is chemically similar to the medications we use to treat ADD.) Finally, people with ADD sometimes also self-medicate with excessive alcohol or other substances.

On the positive side, those with ADD usually possess rare talents and gifts. Those gifts often go unnoticed or undeveloped, however, because of the problems caused by the condition's negative symptoms. ADD sufferers can be remarkably creative and original. They are unusually persistent under certain circumstances and often possess an entrepreneurial flair. They display ingenuity and encourage that trait in others. They tend to improvise well under pressure. Because they have the ability to field multiple inputs simultaneously, they can be strong leaders during times of change. They also tend to rebound quickly after setbacks and bring fresh energy to the company every day.

Executives with ADD typically achieve inconsistent results. Sometimes they fail miserably because they're disorganized and make mistakes. At other times, they perform brilliantly, offering original ideas and strategies that lead to performance at the highest level.

David Neeleman, the CEO of JetBlue Airways, has ADD. School was torture; unable to focus, he hated to study and procrastinated endlessly. "I felt like I should be out doing things, moving things along, but here I was, stuck studying statistics, which I knew had no application to my life," Neeleman told me. "I knew I had to have an education, but at the first opportunity to start a business, I just blew out of college." He climbed quickly in the corporate world, making use of his strengths—original thinking, high energy, an ability to draw out the best in people—and getting help with organization and time management.

Like most people with ADD, Neeleman could sometimes offend with his blunt words, but his ideas were good enough to change the airline industry. For example, he invented the electronic ticket. "When I proposed that idea, people laughed at me, saying no one would go to the airport without a paper ticket," he says. "Now everyone does, and it has saved the industry millions of dollars." It seems fitting that someone with ADD would invent a way around having to remember to bring a paper ticket. Neeleman believes ADD is one of the keys to his success. Far from regretting having it, he celebrates it. But he understands that he must manage his ADD carefully.

Attention deficit trait is characterized by ADD's negative symptoms. Rather than being rooted in genetics, however, ADT is purely a response to the hyperkinetic environment in which we live. Indeed, modern culture all but requires many of us to develop ADT. Never in history has the human brain been asked to track so many data points. Everywhere, people rely on their cell phones, e-mail, and digital assistants in the race to gather and transmit data, plans, and ideas faster and faster. One could argue that the chief value of the modern era is speed, which the novelist Milan Kundera described as "the form of ecstasy that technology has bestowed upon modern man." Addicted to speed, we demand it even when we can't possibly go faster. James Gleick wryly noted in *Faster: The Acceleration of Just About Everything* that the "close door" button in elevators is often the one with the paint worn off. As the human brain struggles to keep up, it falters and then falls into the world of ADT.

This Is Your Brain

While brain scans cannot display anatomical differences between people with "normal" brains and people suffering from ADT, studies have shown that as the human brain is asked to process dizzying amounts of data, its ability to solve problems flexibly and creatively declines and the number of mistakes increases. To find out why, let's go on a brief neurological journey.

Blessed with the largest cortex in all of nature, owners of this trillion-celled organ today put singular pressure on the frontal and prefrontal lobes, which I'll refer to in this article as simply the frontal lobes. This region governs what is called, aptly enough, executive functioning (EF). EF guides decision making and planning; the organization and prioritization of information and ideas; time management; and various other sophisticated, uniquely human, managerial tasks. As long as our frontal lobes remain in charge, everything is fine.

Beneath the frontal lobes lie the parts of the brain devoted to survival. These deep centers govern basic functions like sleep, hunger, sexual desire, breathing, and heart rate, as well as crudely positive and negative emotions. When you are doing well and operating at peak level, the deep centers send up messages of excitement, satisfaction, and joy. They pump up your motivation, help you maintain attention, and don't interfere with working memory, the number of data points you can keep track of at once. But when you are confronted with the sixth decision after the fifth interruption in the midst of a search for the ninth missing piece of information on the day that the third deal has collapsed and the 12th impossible request has blipped unbidden across your computer screen, your brain begins to panic, reacting just as if that sixth decision were a bloodthirsty, man-eating tiger.

As a specialist in learning disabilities, I have found that the most dangerous disability is not any formally diagnosable condition like dyslexia or ADD. It is fear. Fear shifts us into survival mode and thus prevents fluid learning and nuanced understanding. Certainly, if a real tiger is about to attack you, survival is the mode you want to be in. But if you're trying to deal intelligently with a subtle task, survival mode is highly unpleasant and counterproductive.

When the frontal lobes approach capacity and we begin to fear that we can't keep up, the relationship between the higher and lower regions of the brain takes an ominous turn. Thousands of years of evolution have taught the higher brain not to ignore the lower brain's distress signals. In survival mode, the deep areas of the brain assume control and begin to direct the higher regions. As a result, the whole brain gets caught in a neurological catch-22. The deep regions interpret the messages of overload they receive from the frontal lobes in the same way they interpret everything: primitively. They furiously fire signals of fear, anxiety, impatience, irritability, anger, or panic. These alarm signals shanghai the attention of the frontal lobes, forcing them to forfeit much of their power. Because survival signals are irresistible, the frontal lobes get stuck sending messages back to the deep centers saying, "Message received. Trying to work on it but without success." These messages further perturb the deep centers, which send even more powerful messages of distress back up to the frontal lobes.

Meanwhile, in response to what's going on in the brain, the rest of the body—particularly the endocrine, respiratory, cardiovascular, musculoskeletal, and peripheral nervous systems—has shifted into crisis mode and changed its baseline physiology from peace and quiet to red alert. The brain and body are locked in a reverberating circuit while the frontal lobes lose their sophistication, as if vinegar were added to wine. In this state, EF reverts to simpleminded black-and-white thinking; perspective and shades of gray disappear. Intelligence dims. In a futile attempt to do more than is possible, the brain paradoxically reduces its ability to think clearly.

This neurological event occurs when a manager is desperately trying to deal with more input than he possibly can. In survival mode, the manager makes impulsive judgments, angrily rushing to bring closure to whatever matter is at hand. He feels compelled to get the problem under control immediately, to extinguish the perceived danger lest it destroy him. He is robbed of his flexibility, his sense of humor, his ability to deal with the unknown. He forgets the big picture and the goals and values he stands for. He loses his creativity and his ability to change plans. He desperately wants to kill the metaphorical tiger. At these moments he is prone to melting down, to throwing a tantrum, to blaming others, and to sabotaging himself. Or he may go in the opposite direction, falling into denial and total avoidance of the problems attacking him, only to be devoured. This is ADT at its worst.

Though ADT does not always reach such extreme proportions, it does wreak havoc among harried workers. Because no two brains are alike, some people deal with the condition better than others. Regardless of how well executives appear to function, however, no one has total control over his or her executive functioning.

Managing ADT

Unfortunately, top management has so far viewed the symptoms of ADT through the distorting lens of morality or character. Employees who seem unable to keep up the pace are seen as deficient or weak. Consider the case of an executive who came to see me when he was completely overloaded. I suggested he talk the situation over with his superior and ask for help. When my client did so, he was told that if he couldn't handle the work, he ought to think about resigning. Even though his performance assessments were stellar and he'd earned praise for being one of the most creative people in the organization, he was allowed to leave. Because the firm sought to preserve the myth that no straw would ever break its people's backs, it could not tolerate the manager's stating that his back was breaking. After he went out on his own, he flourished.

How can we control the rampaging effects of ADT, both in ourselves and in our organizations? While ADD often requires medication, the treatment of ADT certainly does not. ADT can be controlled only by creatively engineering one's environment and one's emotional and physical health. I have found that the following preventive measures go a long way toward helping executives control their symptoms of ADT.

Promote positive emotions

The most important step in controlling ADT is not to buy a superturbocharged BlackBerry and fill it up with to-dos but rather to create an environment in which the brain can function at its best. This means building a positive, fear-free emotional atmosphere, because emotion is the on/off switch for executive functioning.

There are neurological reasons why ADT occurs less in environments where people are in physical contact and where they trust and respect one another. When you comfortably connect with a colleague, even if you are dealing with an overwhelming problem, the deep centers of the brain send messages through the pleasure center to the area that assigns resources to the frontal lobes. Even when you're under extreme stress, this sense of human connection causes executive functioning to hum.

By contrast, people who work in physical isolation are more likely to suffer from ADT, for the more isolated we are, the more stressed we become. I witnessed a dramatic example of the danger of a disconnected environment and the healing power of a connected one when I consulted for one of the world's foremost university chemistry departments. In the department's formerly hard-driven culture, ADT was rampant, exacerbated by an ethic that forbade anyone to ask for help or even state that anything was wrong. People did not trust one another; they worked on projects alone, which led to more mistrust. Most people were in emotional pain, but implicit in the department's culture was the notion that great pain led to great gain.

In the late 1990s, one of the department's most gifted graduate students killed himself. His suicide note explicitly blamed the university for pushing him past his limit. The department's culture was literally lethal.

Instead of trying to sweep the tragedy under the rug, the chair of the department and his successor acted boldly and creatively. They immediately changed the structure of the supervisory system so that each graduate student and postdoc was assigned three supervisors, rather than a single one with a death grip on the trainee's career. The department set up informal biweekly buffets that allowed people to connect. (Even the most reclusive chemist came out of hiding for food, one of life's great connectors.) The department heads went as far as changing the architecture of the department's main building, taking down walls and adding common areas and an espresso bar complete with a grand piano. They provided lectures and written information to all students about the danger signs of mental wear and tear and offered confidential procedures for students who needed help. These steps, along with regular meetings that included senior faculty and university administrators, led to a more humane, productive culture in which the students and faculty felt fully engaged. The department's performance remained first-rate, and creative research blossomed.

The bottom line is this: Fostering connections and reducing fear promote brainpower. When you make time at least every four to six hours for a "human moment," a face-to-face exchange with a person you like, you are giving your brain what it needs.

Take physical care of your brain

Sleep, a good diet, and exercise are critical for staving off ADT. Though this sounds like a no-brainer, too many of us abuse our brains by neglecting obvious principles of care.

You may try to cope with ADT by sleeping less, in the vain hope that you can get more done. This is the opposite of what you need to do, for ADT sets in when you don't get enough sleep. There is ample documentation to suggest that sleep deprivation engenders a host of problems, from impaired decision making and reduced creativity to reckless behavior and paranoia. We vary in how much sleep we require; a good rule of thumb is that you're getting enough sleep if you can wake up without an alarm clock.

Diet also plays a crucial role in brain health. Many hardworking people habitually inhale carbohydrates, which cause blood glucose levels to yo-yo. This leads to a vicious cycle: Rapid fluctuations in insulin levels further increase the craving for carbohydrates. The brain, which relies on glucose for energy, is left either glutted or gasping, neither of which makes for optimal cognitive functioning.

The brain does much better if the blood glucose level can be held relatively stable. To do this, avoid simple carbohydrates containing sugar and white flour (pastries, white bread, and pasta, for example). Rely on the complex carbohydrates found in fruits, whole grains, and vegetables. Protein is important: Instead of starting your day with coffee and a Danish, try tea and an egg or a piece of smoked salmon on wheat toast. Take a multivitamin every day as well as supplementary omega-3 fatty acids, an excellent source of which is fish oil. The omega-3s and the E and B complex contained in multivitamins promote healthy brain function and may even stave off Alzheimer's disease and inflammatory ills (which can be the starting point for major killers like heart disease, stroke, diabetes, and cancer). Moderate your intake of alcohol, too, because too much kills brain cells and accelerates the development of memory loss and even dementia. As you change your diet to promote optimal brain function and good general health, your body will also shed excess pounds.

If you think you can't afford the time to exercise, think again. Sitting at a desk for hours on end decreases mental acuity, not only because of reduced blood flow to the brain but for other biochemical reasons as well. Physical exercise induces the body to produce an array of chemicals that the brain loves, including endorphins, serotonin, dopamine, epinephrine, and norepinephrine, as well as two recently discovered compounds, brain-derived neurotrophic factor (BDNF) and nerve growth factor (NGF). Both BDNF and NGF promote cell health and development in the brain, stave off the ravages of aging and stress, and keep the brain in tip-top condition. Nothing stimulates the production of BDNF and NGF as robustly as physical exercise, which explains why those who exercise regularly talk about the letdown and sluggishness they experience if they miss their exercise for a few days. You will more than compensate for the time you invest on the treadmill with improved productivity and efficiency. To fend off the symptoms of ADT while you're at work, get up from your desk and go up and down a flight of stairs a few times or walk briskly down a hallway. These quick, simple efforts will push your brain's reset button.

Organize for ADT

It's important to develop tactics for getting organized, but not in the sense of empty New Year's resolutions. Rather, your goal is to order your work in a way that suits you, so that disorganization does not keep you from reaching your goals.

First, devise strategies to help your frontal lobes stay in control. These might include breaking down large tasks into smaller ones and keeping a section of your work space or desk clear at all times. (You do not need to have a neat office, just a neat section of your office.) Similarly, you might try keeping a portion of your day free of appointments, e-mail, and other distractions so that you have time to think and plan. Because e-mail is a wonderful way to procrastinate and set yourself up for ADT at the same time, you might consider holding specific "e-mail hours," since it isn't necessary to reply to every e-mail right away.

When you start your day, don't allow yourself to get sucked into vortices of e-mail or voice mail or into attending to minor tasks that eat up your time but don't pack a punch. Attend to a critical task instead. Before you leave for the day, make a list of no more than five priority items that will require your attention tomorrow. Short lists force you to prioritize and complete your tasks. Additionally, keep torrents of documents at bay. One of my patients, an executive with ADD, uses the OHIO rule: Only handle it once. If he touches a document, he acts on it, files it, or throws it away. "I don't put it in a pile," he says. "Piles are like weeds. If you let them grow, they take over everything."

Pay attention to the times of day when you feel that you perform at your best; do your most important work then and save the rote work for other times. Set up your office in a way that helps mental functioning. If you focus better with music, have music (if need be, use earphones). If you think best on your feet, work standing up or walk around frequently. If doodling or drumming your fingers helps, figure out a way to do so without bothering anyone, or get a fidget toy to bring to meetings. These small strategies sound mundane, but they address the ADT devil that resides in distracting details.

Protect your frontal lobes

To stay out of survival mode and keep your lower brain from usurping control, slow down. Take the time you need to comprehend what is going on, to listen, to ask questions, and to digest what's been said so that you don't get confused and send your brain into panic. Empower an assistant to ride herd on you; insist that he or she tell you to stop e-mailing, get off the telephone, or leave the office.

Control Your ADT

In General

- Get adequate sleep.

- Watch what you eat. Avoid simple, sugary carbohydrates, moderate your intake of alcohol, add protein, stick to complex carbohydrates (vegetables, whole grains, fruit).

- Exercise at least 30 minutes at least every other day.

- Take a daily multivitamin and an omega-3 fatty acid supplement.

At Work

- Do all you can to create a trusting, connected work environment.

- Have a friendly, face-to-face talk with a person you like every four to six hours.

- Break large tasks into smaller ones.

- Keep a section of your work space or desk clear at all times.

- Each day, reserve some "think time" that's free from appointments, e-mail, and phone calls.

- Set aside e-mail until you've completed at least one or two more important tasks.

If you do begin to feel overwhelmed, try the following mind-clearing tricks. Do an easy rote task, such as resetting the calendar on your watch or writing a memo on a neutral topic. If you feel anxious about beginning a project, pull out a sheet of paper or fire up your word processor and write a paragraph about something unrelated to the project (a description of your house, your car, your shoes—anything you know well). You can also tackle the easiest part of the task; for example, write just the title of a memo about it. Open a dictionary and read a few definitions, or spend five minutes doing a crossword puzzle. Each of these little tasks quiets your lower brain by tricking it into shutting off alarmist messages and puts your frontal lobes back in full control.

- Before you leave work each day, create a short list of three to five items you will attend to the next day.

- Try to act on, file, or toss every document you touch.

- Don't let papers accumulate.

- Pay attention to the times of day when you feel that you are at your best; do your most important work then, and save the rote work for other times.

- Do whatever you need to do to work in a more focused way: Add background music, walk around, and so on.

- Ask a colleague or an assistant to help you stop talking on the telephone, e-mailing, or working too late.

When You Feel Overwhelmed

- Slow down.

- Do an easy rote task: Reset your watch, write a note about a neutral topic (such as a description of your house), read a few dictionary definitions, do a short crossword puzzle.

- Move around: Go up and down a flight of stairs or walk briskly.

- Ask for help, delegate a task, or brainstorm with a colleague. In short, do not worry alone.

Finally, be ready for the next attack of ADT by posting the sidebar "Control Your ADT" near your desk where you can see it. Knowing that you are prepared diminishes the likelihood of an attack, because you're not susceptible to panic.

What Leaders Can Do

All too often, companies induce and exacerbate ADT in their employees by demanding fast thinking rather than deep thinking. Firms also ask employees to work on multiple overlapping projects and initiatives, resulting in second-rate thinking. Worse, companies that ask their employees to do too much at once tend to reward those who say yes to overload while punishing those who choose to focus and say no.

Moreover, organizations make the mistake of forcing their employees to do more and more with less and less by eliminating support staff. Such companies end up losing money in the long run, for the more time a manager has to spend being his own administrative assistant and the less he is able to delegate, the less effective he will be in doing the important work of moving the organization forward. Additionally, firms that ignore the symptoms of ADT in their employees suffer its ill effects: Employees underachieve, create clutter, cut corners, make careless mistakes, and squander their brainpower. As demands continue to increase, a toxic, high-pressure environment leads to high rates of employee illness and turnover.

To counteract ADT and harness employee brainpower, firms should invest in amenities that contribute to a positive atmosphere. One company that has done an excellent job in this regard is SAS Institute, a major software company in North Carolina. The company famously offers its employees a long list of perks: a 36,000-square-foot, on-site gym; a seven-hour workday that ends at 5 PM; the largest on-site day care facility in North Carolina; a cafeteria that provides baby seats and high chairs so parents can eat lunch with their children; unlimited sick days; and much more. The atmosphere at SAS is warm, connected, and relaxed. The effect on the bottom line is profoundly positive; turnover is never higher than 5%. The company saves the millions other software companies spend on recruiting, training, and severance (estimated to be at least 1.5 times salary in the software industry). Employees return the favors with high productivity. The forces of ADT that shred other organizations never gain momentum at SAS.

Leaders can also help prevent ADT by matching employees' skills to tasks. When managers assign goals that stretch people too far or ask workers to focus on what they're not good at rather than what they do well, stress rises. By contrast, managers who understand the dangers of ADT can find ways of keeping themselves and their organizations on track. JetBlue's David Neeleman, for example, has shamelessly and publicly identified what he is not good at and found ways to deal with his shortcomings, either by delegating or by empowering his assistant to direct him. Neeleman also models this behavior for everyone else in the organization. His openness about the challenges of his ADD gives others permission to speak about their own attention deficit difficulties and to garner the support they need. He also encourages his managers to match people with tasks that fit their cognitive and emotional styles, knowing that no one style is best. Neeleman believes that helping people work to their strengths is not just a mark of sophisticated management; it's also an excellent way to boost worker productivity and morale.

ADT is a very real threat to all of us. If we do not manage it, it manages us. But an understanding of ADT and its ravages allows us to apply practical methods to improve our work and our lives. In the end, the most critical step an enlightened leader can take to address the problem of ADT is to name it. Bringing ADT out of the closet and describing its symptoms removes the stigma and eliminates the moral condemnation companies have for so long mistakenly leveled at overburdened employees. By giving people permission to ask for help and remaining vigilant for signs of stress, organizations will go a long way toward fostering more productive, well-balanced, and intelligent work environments.

Originally published in January 2005. Reprint R0501E

Be a Better Leader, Have a Richer Life

by Stewart D. Friedman

IN MY RESEARCH AND COACHING WORK over the past two decades, I have met many people who feel unfulfilled, overwhelmed, or stagnant because they are forsaking performance in one or more aspects of their lives. They aren't bringing their leadership abilities to bear in all of life's domains—work, home, community, and self (mind, body, and spirit). Of course, there will always be some tension among the different roles we play. But, contrary to the common wisdom, there's no reason to assume that it's a zero-sum game. It makes more sense to pursue excellent performance as a leader in all four domains—achieving what I call "four-way wins"—not trading off one for another but finding mutual value among them.

This is the main idea in a program called Total Leadership that I teach at the Wharton School and at companies and workshops around the world. "Total" because it's about the whole person and "Leadership" because it's about creating sustainable change to benefit not just you but the most important people around you.

Scoring four-way wins starts by taking a clear view of what you want from and can contribute to each domain of your life, now and in the future, with thoughtful consideration of the people who matter most to you and the expectations you have for one another. This is followed by systematically designing and implementing carefully crafted experiments—doing something new for a short period to see how it affects all four domains. If an experiment doesn't work out, you stop or adjust, and little is lost. If it does work out, it's a small win; over time these add up so that your overall efforts are focused increasingly on what and who matter most. Either way, you learn more about how to lead in all parts of your life.

This process doesn't require inordinate risk. On the contrary, it works because it entails realistic expectations, short-term changes that are in your control, and the explicit support of those around you. Take, for instance, Kenneth Chen, a manager I met at a workshop in 2005. (All names in this article are pseudonyms.) His professional goal was to become CEO, but he had other goals as well, which on the face of it might have appeared conflicting. He had recently moved to Philadelphia and wanted to get more involved with his community. He also wished to strengthen bonds with his family. To further all of these goals, he decided to join a city-based community board, which would not only allow him to hone his leadership skills (in support of his professional goal) but also have benefits in the family domain. It would give him more in common with his sister, a teacher who gave back to the community every day, and he hoped his fiancée would participate as well, enabling them to do something together for the greater good. He would feel more spiritually alive and this, in turn, would increase his self-confidence at work.

Now, about three years later, he reports that he is not only on a community board with his fiancée but also on the formal succession track for CEO. He's a better leader in all aspects of his life because he is acting in ways that are more consistent with his values. He is creatively enhancing his performance in all domains of his life and leading others to improve their performance by encouraging them to better integrate the different parts of their lives, too.

Kenneth is not alone. Workshop participants assess themselves at the beginning and the end of the program, and they consistently report improvements in their effectiveness, as well as a greater sense of harmony among the once-competing domains of their lives. In a study over a four-month period of more than 300 business professionals

Idea in Brief

Life's a zero-sum game, right? The more you strive to win in one dimension (e.g., your work), the more the other three dimensions (your self, your home, and your community) must lose. Not according to Friedman. You don't have to make trade-offs among life's domains. Nor should you: trading off can leave you feeling exhausted, unfulfilled, or isolated. And it hurts the people you care about most.

To excel in all dimensions of life, use Friedman's **Total Leadership** process. First, articulate who and what matters most in your life.

Then experiment with small changes that enhance your satisfaction and performance in *all four domains*. For example, exercising three mornings a week gives you more energy for work and improves your self-esteem and health, which makes you a better parent and friend.

Friedman's research suggests that people who focus on the concept of Total Leadership have a 20%–39% increase in satisfaction in all life domains, and a 9% improvement in job performance—even while working shorter weeks.

(whose average age was about 35), their *satisfaction* increased by an average of 20% in their work lives, 28% in their home lives, and 31% in their community lives. Perhaps most significant, their satisfaction in the domain of the self—their physical and emotional health and their intellectual and spiritual growth—increased by 39%. But they also reported that their *performance* improved: at work (by 9%), at home (15%), in the community (12%), and personally (25%). Paradoxically, these gains were made even as participants spent less time on work and more on other aspects of their lives. They're working smarter—and they're more focused, passionate, and committed to what they're doing.

While hundreds of leaders at all levels go through this program every year, you don't need a workshop to identify worthwhile experiments. The process is pretty straightforward, though not simple. In the sections that follow, I will give you an overview of the process and take you through the basics of designing and implementing experiments to produce four-way wins.

Idea in Practice

Total Leadership helps you mitigate a range of problems that stem from making trade-offs among the different dimensions of your life:

- Feeling **unfulfilled** because you're not doing what you love

- Feeling **inauthentic** because you're not acting according to your values

- Feeling **disconnected** from people who matter to you

- Feeling **exhausted** by trying to keep up with it all

To tackle such problems using Total Leadership, take these steps.

1. Reflect

For each of the four domains of your life—work, home, community, and self, reflect on how important each is to you, how much time and energy you devote to each, and how satisfied you are in each. Are there discrepancies between what is important to you and how you spend your time and energy? What is your overall life satisfaction?

2. Brainstorm Possibilities

Based on the insights you've achieved during your four-way reflection, brainstorm a long list of small experiments that may help you move closer to greater satisfaction in all four domains. These are new ways of doing things that would carry minimal risk and let you see results quickly. For example:

- Turning off cell phones during family dinners could help you sharpen your focus on the people who matter most to you.

- Exercising several times a week could give you more energy.

- Joining a club with coworkers could help you forge closer friendships with them.

- Preparing for the week ahead on Sunday evenings could help you sleep better and go into the new week refreshed.

3. Choose Experiments

Narrow the list of experiments you've brainstormed to the three most promising. They should:

The Total Leadership Process

The Total Leadership concept rests on three principles:

- Be real: Act with authenticity by clarifying what's important.

- Be whole: Act with integrity by respecting the whole person.

- Improve your satisfaction and performance in all four dimensions of your life.

- Have effects viewed as positive by the people who matter to you in every dimension of your life.

- Be the most costly—in regret and missed opportunities—if you *don't* do them.

- Position you to practice skills you most want to develop and do more of what you *want* to be doing.

4. Measure Progress

Develop a scorecard for each experiment you've chosen. For example:

Experiment: Exercise three mornings a week with spouse.

Life dimension	Experiment's goals	How I will measure success	Implementation steps
Work	Improved alertness and productivity	No caffeine to get through the day; more productive sales calls	• Get doctor's feedback on exercise plan. • Join gym. • Set alarm earlier on exercise days. • Tell coworkers, family, and friends about my plan, how I need their help, and how it will benefit them.
Home	Increased closeness with spouse	Fewer arguments with spouse	
Community	Greater strength to participate in athletic fundraising events with friends	Three 10K fundraising walks completed by end of year	
Self	Improved self-esteem	Greater confidence	

- Be innovative: Act with creativity by experimenting with how things get done.

You begin the process by thinking, writing, and talking with peer coaches to identify your core values, your leadership vision, and the current alignment of your actions and values—clarifying what's important. Peer coaching is enormously valuable, at this stage and throughout, because an outside perspective provides a sounding board for your ideas, challenges you, gives you a fresh way to see the possibilities for innovation, and helps hold you accountable to your commitments.

You then identify the most important people—"key stakeholders"—in all domains and the performance expectations you have of one another. Then you talk with them: If you're like most participants, you'll be surprised to find that what, and how much, your key stakeholders actually need from you is different from, and less than, what you thought beforehand.

These insights create opportunities for you to focus your attention more intelligently, spurring innovative action. Now, with a firmer grounding in what's most important, and a more complete picture of your inner circle, you begin to see new ways of making life better, not just for you but for the people around you.

The next step is to design experiments and then try them out during a controlled period of time. The best experiments are changes that your stakeholders wish for as much as, if not more than, you do.

Designing Experiments

To pursue a four-way win means to produce a change intended to fulfill multiple goals that benefit each and every domain of your life. In the domain of work, typical goals for an experiment can be captured under these broad headings: taking advantage of new opportunities for increasing productivity, reducing hidden costs, and improving the work environment. Goals for home and community tend to revolve around improving relationships and contributing more to society. For the self, it's usually about improving health and finding greater meaning in life.

As you think through the goals for your experiment, keep in mind the interests and opinions of your key stakeholders and anyone else who might be affected by the changes you are envisioning. In exploring the idea of joining a community board, for instance, Kenneth Chen sought advice from his boss, who had served on many boards, and also from the company's charitable director and the vice president of talent. In this way, he got their support. His employers could see how his participation on a board would benefit the company by developing Kenneth's leadership skills and his social network.

Some experiments benefit only a single domain directly while having indirect benefits in the others. For example, setting aside three mornings a week to exercise improves your health directly but may indirectly give you more energy for your work and raise your self-esteem, which in turn might make you a better father and friend. Other activities—such as running a half-marathon with your kids to raise funds for a charity sponsored by your company—occur in, and directly benefit, all four domains simultaneously. Whether the benefits are direct or indirect, achieving a four-way win is the goal. That's what makes the changes sustainable: Everyone benefits. The expected gains need not accrue until sometime in the future, so keep in mind that some benefits may not be obvious—far-off career advancements, for instance, or a contact who might ultimately offer valuable connections.

Identify possibilities

Open your mind to what's possible and try to think of as many potential experiments as you can, describing in a sentence or two what you would do in each. This is a time to let your imagination run free. Don't worry about all the potential obstacles at this point.

At first blush, conceiving of experiments that produce benefits for all the different realms may seem a formidable task. After all, if it were easy, people wouldn't be feeling so much tension between work and the rest of their lives. But I've found that most people realize it's not that hard once they approach the challenge systematically. And, like a puzzle, it can be fun, especially if you keep in mind that experiments must fit your particular circumstances. Experiments can and do take myriad forms. But having sifted through hundreds of experiment designs, my research team and I have found that they tend to fall into nine general types. Use the nine categories described in the exhibit "How Can I Design an Experiment to Improve All Domains of My Life?" to organize your thinking.

How can I design an experiment to improve all domains of my life?

Our research has revealed that most successful experiments combine components of nine general categories. Thinking about possibilities in this way will make it easier for you to conceive of the small changes you can make that will mutually benefit your work, your home, your community, and yourself. Most experiments are a hybrid of some combination of these categories.

Tracking and Reflecting

Keeping a record of activities, thoughts, and feelings (and perhaps distributing it to friends, family, and coworkers) to assess progress on personal and professional goals, thereby increasing self-awareness and maintaining priorities.

Examples

- Record visits to the gym along with changes in energy levels
- Track the times of day when you feel most engaged or most lethargic

Planning and Organizing

Taking actions designed to better use time and prepare and plan for the future.

Examples

- Use a PDA for all activities, not just work
- Share your schedule with someone else
- Prepare for the week on Sunday evening

Rejuvenating and Restoring

Attending to body, mind, and spirit so that the tasks of daily living and working are undertaken with renewed power, focus, and commitment.

Examples

- Quit unhealthy physical habits (smoking, drinking)
- Make time for reading a novel
- Engage in activities that improve emotional and spiritual health (yoga, meditation, etc.)

Appreciating and Caring

Having fun with people (typically, by doing things with coworkers outside work), caring for others, and appreciating relationships as a way of bonding at a basic human level to respect the whole person, which increases trust.

Examples

- Join a book group or health club with coworkers
- Help your son complete his homework
- Devote one day a month to community service

Focusing and Concentrating

Being physically present, psychologically present, or both when needed to pay attention to stakeholders who matter most. Sometimes this means saying no to opportunities or obligations. Includes attempts to show more respect to important people encountered in different domains and the need to be accessible to them.

Examples

- Turn off digital communication devices at a set time
- Set aside a specific time to focus on one thing or person
- Review e-mail at preset times during the day

Revealing and Engaging

Sharing more of yourself with others—and listening—so they can better support your values and the steps you want to take toward your leadership vision. By enhancing communication about different aspects of life, you demonstrate respect for the whole person.

Examples

- Have weekly conversations about religion with spouse
- Describe your vision to others
- Mentor a new employee

Time Shifting and "Re-Placing"

Working remotely or during different hours to increase flexibility and thus better fit in community, family, and personal activities while increasing efficiency; questioning traditional assumptions and trying new ways to get things done.

Examples

- Work from home
- Take music lessons during your lunch hour
- Do work during your commute

Delegating and Developing

Reallocating tasks in ways that increase trust, free up time, and develop skills in yourself and others; working smarter by reducing or eliminating low-priority activities.

(continued)

Examples

- Hire a personal assistant
- Have a subordinate take on some of your responsibilities

Exploring and Venturing

Taking steps toward a new job, career, or other activity that better aligns your work, home, community, and self with your core values and aspirations.

Examples

- Take on new roles at work, such as a cross-functional assignment
- Try a new coaching style
- Join the board of your child's day care center

One category of experiment involves changes in where and when work gets done. One workshop participant, a sales director for a global cement producer, tried working online from his local public library one day a week to free himself from his very long commute. This was a break from a company culture that didn't traditionally support employees working remotely, but the change benefited everyone. He had more time for outside interests, and he was more engaged and productive at work.

Another category has to do with regular self-reflection. As an example, you might keep a record of your activities, thoughts, and feelings over the course of a month to see how various actions influence your performance and quality of life. Still another category focuses on planning and organizing your time—such as trying out a new technology that coordinates commitments at work with those in the other domains.

Conversations about work and the rest of life tend to emphasize segmentation: How do I shut out the office when I am with my family? How can I eliminate distractions and concentrate purely on work? But, in some cases, it might be better to make boundaries between domains more permeable, not thicker. The very technologies that make it hard for us to maintain healthy boundaries among domains also enable us to blend them in ways—unfathomable even a decade ago—that can render us more productive and more ful-filled. These tools give us choices. The challenge we all face is learning how to use them wisely, and smart experiments give you an opportunity to increase your skill in doing so. The main point is to identify possibilities that will work well in your unique situation.

All effective experiments require that you question traditional assumptions about how things get done, as the sales director did. It's easier to feel free to do this, and to take innovative action, when you know that your goal is to improve performance in all domains and that you'll be gathering data about the impact of your experiment to determine if indeed it is working—for your key stakeholders and for you.

Whatever type you choose, the most useful experiments feel like something of a stretch: not too easy, not too daunting. It might be something quite mundane for someone else, but that doesn't matter. What's critical is that *you* see it as a moderately difficult challenge.

Choose a few, get started, and adapt

Coming up with possibilities is an exercise in unbounded imagination. But when it comes time to take action, it's not practical to try out more than three experiments at once. Typically, two turn out to be relatively successful and one goes haywire, so you will earn some small wins, and learn something useful about leadership, without biting off more than you can chew. Now the priority is to narrow the list to the three most-promising candidates by reviewing which will:

- Give you the best overall return on your investment

- Be the most costly in regret and missed opportunities if you don't do it

- Allow you to practice the leadership skills you most want to develop

- Be the most fun by involving more of what you want to be doing

- Move you furthest toward your vision of how you want to lead your life

Once you choose and begin to move down the road with your experiment, however, be prepared to adapt to the unforeseen. Don't become too wedded to the details of any one experiment's plan, because you will at some point be surprised and need to adjust. An executive I'll call Lim, for example, chose as one experiment to run the Chicago Marathon. He had been feeling out of shape, which in turn diminished his energy and focus both at work and at home. His wife, Joanne, was pregnant with their first child and initially supported the plan because she believed that the focus required by the training and the physical outlet it provided would make Lim a better father. The family also had a strong tradition of athleticism, and Joanne herself was an accomplished athlete. Lim was training with his boss and other colleagues, and all agreed that it would be a healthy endeavor that would improve professional communication (as they thought there would be plenty of time to bond during training).

But as her delivery date approached, Joanne became apprehensive, which she expressed to Lim as concern that he might get injured. Her real concern, though, was that he was spending so much time on an activity that might drain his energy at a point when the family needed him most. One adjustment that Lim made to reassure Joanne of his commitment to their family was to initiate another experiment in which he took the steps needed to allow him to work at home on Thursday afternoons. He had to set up some new technologies and agree to send a monthly memo to his boss summarizing what he was accomplishing on those afternoons. He also bought a baby sling, which would allow him to keep his new son with him while at home.

In the end, not only were Joanne and their baby on hand to cheer Lim on while he ran the marathon, but she ended up joining him for the second half of the race to give him a boost when she saw his energy flagging. His business unit's numbers improved during the period when he was training and working at home. So did the unit's morale—people began to see the company as more flexible, and they were encouraged to be more creative in how they got their own work done—and word got around. Executives throughout the firm began to come up with their own ideas for ways to pay more attention to other sides of their employees' lives and so build a stronger sense of community at work.

The investment in a well-designed experiment almost always pays off because you learn how to lead in new and creative ways in all parts of your life. And if your experiments turn out well—as they usually, but not always, do—it will benefit everyone: you, your business, your family, and your community.

Measuring Progress

The only way to fail with an experiment is to fail to learn from it, and this makes useful metrics essential. No doubt it's better to achieve the results you are after than to fall short, but hitting targets does not in itself advance you toward becoming the leader you want to be. Failed experiments give you, and those around you, information that helps create better ones in the future.

The exhibit "How Do I Know If My Experiment Is Working?" shows how Kenneth Chen measured his progress. He used this simple chart to spell out the intended benefits of his experiment in each of the four domains and how he would assess whether he had realized these benefits. To set up your own scorecard, use a separate sheet for each experiment; at the top of the page, write a brief description of it. Then record your goals for each domain in the first column. In the middle column, describe your results metrics: how you will measure whether the goals for each domain have been achieved. In the third column, describe your action metrics—the plan for the steps you will take to implement your experiment. As you begin to implement your plan, you may find that your initial indicators are too broad or too vague, so refine your scorecard as you go along to make it more useful for you. The main point is to have practical ways of measuring your outcomes and your progress toward them, and the approach you take only needs to work for you and your stakeholders.

Workshop participants have used all kinds of metrics: cost savings from reduced travel, number of e-mail misunderstandings averted, degree of satisfaction with family time, hours spent volunteering at a

How do I know if my experiment is working?

Using this tool, an executive I'll call Kenneth Chen systematically set out in detail his various goals, the metrics he would use to measure his progress, and the steps he would take in conducting an experiment that would further those goals—joining the board of a nonprofit organization. Kenneth's work sheet is merely an example: Every person's experiments, goals, and metrics are unique.

A Sample Scorecard

	EXPERIMENT'S GOALS	HOW I WILL MEASURE SUCCESS	IMPLEMENTATION STEPS
Work	▲ To fulfill the expectation that executives will give back to the local community	► Collect business cards from everyone I meet on the board and during board meetings, and keep track of the number of professionals I meet	☐ Meet with my manager, who has sat on many boards and can provide support and advice
	▲ To establish networks with other officers in my company and other professionals in the area	► After each meeting, regularly record the leadership skills of those I would like to emulate	☐ Meet with the director of my company's foundation to determine my real interests and to help assess what relationship our firm has with various community organizations
	▲ To learn leadership skills from other board members and from the organization I join		☐ Discuss my course of action with my fiancée and see whether joining a board interests her
Home	▲ To join a board that can involve my fiancée, Celine	► See whether Celine gets involved in the board	☐ Sign up to attend the December 15 overview session of the Business on Board program
	▲ To have something to discuss with my sister (a special-education instructor)	► Record the number of conversations my sister and I have about community service for the next three months and see whether they have brought us closer	☐ Assess different opportunities within the community and then reach out to organizations I'm interested in

Community

▲ To provide my leadership skills to a nonprofit organization

▲ To get more involved in giving back to the community

Self

▲ To feel good about contributing to others' welfare

▲ To see others grow as a result of my efforts

▲ To become more compassionate

▲ Record what I learn about each nonprofit organization I research

▲ Record the number of times I attend board meetings

▲ Assess how I feel about myself in a daily journal

▲ Assess the effect I have on others in terms of potential number of people affected

▲ Ask for feedback from others about whether I've become more compassionate

☐ Apply for membership to a community board

teen center, and so on. Metrics may be objective or subjective, qual-itative or quantitative, reported by you or by others, and frequently or intermittently observed. When it comes to frequency, for in-stance, it helps to consider how long you'll be able to remember what you did. For example, if you were to go on a diet to get health-ier, increase energy, and enhance key relationships, food intake would be an important metric. But would you be able to remember what you ate two days ago?

Small Wins for Big Change

Experiments shouldn't be massive, all-encompassing shifts in the way you live. Highly ambitious designs usually fail because they're too much to handle. The best experiments let you try something new while minimizing the inevitable risks associated with change. When the stakes are smaller, it's easier to overcome the fear of fail-ure that inhibits innovation. You start to see results, and others take note, which both inspires you to go further and builds support from your key stakeholders.

Another benefit of the small-wins approach to experiments is that it opens doors that would otherwise be closed. You can say to people invested in the decision, "Let's just try this. If it doesn't work, we'll go back to the old way or try something different." By framing an ex-periment as a trial, you reduce resistance because people are more likely to try something new if they know it's not permanent and if they have control over deciding whether the experiment is working according to *their* performance expectations.

But "small" is a relative term—what might look like a small step for you could seem like a giant leap to me, and vice versa. So don't get hung up on the word. What's more, this isn't about the scope or impor-tance of the changes you eventually make. Large-scale change is grounded in small steps toward a big idea. So while the steps in an ex-periment might be small, the goals are not. Ismail, a successful 50-year-old entrepreneur and CEO of an engineering services com-pany, described the goal for his first experiment this way: "Restructure my company and my role in it." There's nothing small about that. He felt he was missing a sense of purpose.

Ismail designed practical steps that would allow him to move toward his large goal over time. His first experiments were small and achievable. He introduced a new method that both his colleagues and his wife could use to communicate with him. He began to hold sacrosanct time for his family and his church. As he looked for ways to free up more time, he initiated delegation experiments that had the effect of flattening his organization's structure. These small wins crossed over several domains, and eventually he did indeed transform his company and his own role in it. When I spoke with him 18 months after he'd started, he acknowledged that he'd had a hard time coping with the loss of control over tactical business matters, but he described his experiments as "a testament to the idea of winning the small battles and letting the war be won as a result." He and his leadership team both felt more confident about the firm's new organizational structure.

People try the Total Leadership program for a variety of reasons. Some feel unfulfilled because they're not doing what they love. Some don't feel genuine because they're not acting according to their values. Others feel disconnected, isolated from people who matter to them. They crave stronger relationships, built on trust, and yearn for enriched social networks. Still others are just in a rut. They want to tap into their creative energy but don't know how (and sometimes lack the courage) to do so. They feel out of control and unable to fit in all that's important to them.

My hunch is that there are more four-way wins available to you than you'd think. They are there for the taking. You have to know how to look for them and then find the support and zeal to pursue them. By providing a blueprint for how you can be real, be whole, and be innovative as a leader in all parts of your life, this program helps you perform better according to the standards of the most important people in your life; feel better in all the domains of your life;

and foster greater harmony among the domains by increasing the resources available to you to fit all the parts of your life together. No matter what your career stage or current position, you can be a better leader and have a richer life—if you are ready and willing to rise to the challenge.

Originally published in April 2008. Reprint R0804H

Reclaim Your Job

by Sumantra Ghoshal and Heike Bruch

TASK MOST MANAGERS WHAT GETS in the way of success at work, and you hear the familiar litany of complaints: Not enough time. Shrinking resources. Lack of opportunity. When you look more closely, you begin to see that these are, for the most part, excuses. What gets in the way of managers' success is something much more personal—a deep uncertainty about acting according to their own best judgment. Rather than doing what they really need to do to advance the company's fortunes—and their own careers—they spin their wheels doing what they presume everyone else wants them to do.

Over the past five years, we have studied hundreds of managers as they have gone about their daily work in a variety of settings, including a global airline and a large U.S. oil company. As we demonstrated in "Beware the Busy Manager" (HBR February 2002), fully 90% of the managers we observed wasted their time and frittered away their productivity, despite having well-defined projects, goals, and the knowledge necessary to get their jobs done. Such managers remain trapped in inefficiency because they simply assume that they do not have enough personal discretion or control. The ability to seize initiative is the most essential quality of any truly successful manager.

In most instances, the demands that managers accept as givens are actually discretionary in nature. We have repeatedly confronted in our research a curious but pervasive reality of corporate life: Most managers complain about having too little freedom in their jobs, while their bosses complain about managers' failure to grasp opportunities. The truly effective managers we've observed are purposeful, trust in their own judgment, and adopt long-term, big-picture views to fulfill personal goals that tally with those of the organization as a whole. They break out of their perceived boxes, take control of their jobs, and become more productive by learning to do the following:

Manage demands
Most managers feel overwhelmed by demands. They assume that the business will come to a crashing halt without them and so allow real or imagined day-to-day work demands to subsume their own judgment. Effective managers proactively control their tasks and the expectations of their major stakeholders, which allows them to meet strategic goals rather than fight fires.

Generate resources
By following what they believe are strict orders from the top, many typical managers tend to concentrate on working within budget and resource constraints—thereby developing a boxed-in, "can't do" mind-set. By contrast, effective managers develop inventive strategies for circumventing real or imagined limitations. They map out ways around constraints by developing and acting on long-term strategies, making trade-offs, and occasionally breaking rules to achieve their goals.

Recognize and exploit alternatives
Average managers don't have enough perspective on the company's overall business strategy to present an alternative view. Effective managers, by contrast, develop and use deep expertise about an individual area that dovetails with the company's strategy. This tactic allows them to come up with a variety of innovative approaches to a given situation.[1]

In short, truly effective managers don't operate in the context of individual tasks or jobs but in the much broader context of their organizations and careers. That approach sounds simple enough, but it is sometimes hard to act on because some organizational cultures that

Idea in Brief

90% of managers waste time and fritter away their productivity by grappling with an endless list of demands from others. Why? We assume—wrongly—that those demands are *requirements*, and that we lack personal discretion or control over our jobs. The consequence? We remain trapped in inefficiency.

But we can escape this trap—if we learn how to grasp opportunities, trust our own judgment, and methodically fulfill personal goals that tally with our organizations' objectives. The keys? Set priorities—then stick to them, focusing on

efforts that support those priorities. Overcome resource constraints by attacking goals strategically, demonstrating success at every step. And develop a range of alternatives to exploit when plan A fails.

We all want to make a difference in our organizations, as well as build satisfying careers. By understanding how we inhibit ourselves and taking purposeful, strategic action, we can seize control of our jobs—rather than letting our jobs control us. The payoff? Impressive results for our companies and rewarding work lives for us.

tout "empowerment" actually discourage volition among their managers. Young, high-tech companies, for example, sometimes hold their managers hostage to frenzy, thus inhibiting the reflective and persistent pursuit of long-term goals. Other cultures—particularly those of old and established corporations with command-and-control hierarchies—can encourage people to go along with the status quo, regardless of the level of organizational dysfunction. In both kinds of environments, managers tend to fall into a reactive state of mind, assuming that any initiative they show will be either ignored or discouraged.

In most cases, however, it is not the environment that inhibits managers from taking purposeful action. Rather, it is managers themselves. We have found that managers can learn to act on their own potential and make a difference. Here's how.

Dealing with Demands

Almost everyone complains about not having enough time to deal with all the demands on them, but, in reality, a highly fragmented

Idea in Practice

To reclaim your job and better support your company's priorities, apply three strategies.

Prioritize Demands

To achieve personal and organizational goals quickly, *slow down* and focus your time and attention.

> *Example:* McKinsey associate principal Jessica Spungin took on too many projects that had little connection to her skills and interests. Result? Her project teams rated her second from the bottom among her peers.
>
> Realizing her desire to be indispensable sprang from lack of confidence, Spungin took steps to manage demands. She clarified her goal: to become a partner. Then she set long-term priorities supporting that goal. She began managing her own development; for example, choosing assignments that most interested her. And she started orchestrating her time, meeting only with people who really needed her and working on long-term projects during months when she traveled less.
>
> Her reward? She scored second from the top in her peer group—and was named a McKinsey partner.

Liberate Resources

To relax resource constraints and win the backing you want, attack your goals strategically. Be patient. The process can take years.

> *Example:* As the new head of HR development at airline Lufthansa, Thomas Sattelberger dreamed of launching Germany's first corporate business school. Knowing he needed several years to establish his credibility, he first overhauled inefficient HR processes. He then developed

day is also a very lazy day. It can seem easier to fight fires than to set priorities and stick to them. The truth is that managers who carefully set boundaries and priorities achieve far more than busy ones do.

To beat the busy habit, managers must overcome the psychological desire to be indispensable. Because their work is interactive and interdependent, most managers thrive on their sense of importance to others. When they are not worrying about meeting their superiors' (or their clients') expectations, they fret about their direct reports, often falling victim to the popular fallacy that good bosses initiatives supporting the school, raising money for these projects by presenting compelling facts and arguments to his counterparts and CEO.

After four years of methodical work on Sattelberger's part, Lufthansa's CEO and board understood how his programs fit together. When he wrote a memo to directors requesting creation of the school before Daimler-Benz could beat Lufthansa to the punch, the board promptly approved the request.

Exploit Alternatives

Use your expertise to anticipate—and circumvent—possible obstacles to your goals. You'll expand the scope of opportunity for your company *and* yourself.

Example: Dan Andersson, a manager at oil refiner Conoco-Phillips, was part of a team

exploring Conoco's entrance into the Finnish market. Conoco decided to store petrol in tanks in Finland that Shell had abandoned. But Andersson developed contingency plans. Plan B, for instance, involved building a new facility.

His efforts paid off. When research revealed the abandoned tanks were unsuitable for petrol storage, Andersson activated Plan B. Though the new-facility target site was contaminated, Andersson discovered that Shell was responsible for cleaning the site. Once cleanup ended, Conoco built the tanks.

Conoco became the most efficient operator of automated self-service filling stations in Finland. Andersson now heads Conoco's retail development in Europe.

always make themselves available. At first, managers—particularly novices—seem to thrive on all this clamoring for their time; the busier they are, the more valuable they feel. Inevitably, however, things start to slip. Eventually, many managers simply burn out and fail, not only because they find little time to pursue their own agendas but also because, in trying to please everyone, they typically end up pleasing no one.

Jessica Spungin found herself caught in this trap when she was promoted to associate principal in McKinsey's London office. As an AP, a consultant is expected to take on more responsibilities of the partnership group, juggle multiple projects, serve as a team leader, and play an active role in office life. Spungin dove in to all these tasks headfirst. While she was handling two major client projects, she was asked to jointly lead recruitment for U.K. universities and business schools, participate in an internal research initiative, serve as a senior coach for six business analysts, run an office party for 750 people, get involved in internal training, and help out on a new project for a health care company.

In her first round of feedback from the three project teams she oversaw, she was rated second from the bottom among her peers. Spungin realized that her desire to be indispensable sprang from a lack of confidence. "I never said no to people in case they thought I couldn't cope. I never said no to a client who wanted me to be present at a meeting," she told us. "I did what I thought was expected—regardless of what I was good at, what was important, or what I could physically do."

The first step in Spungin's transformation from a busy to an effective manager was to develop a vision of what she really wanted to achieve at McKinsey: to be named a partner. In developing a clear mental picture of herself in that role, she traded in her habit of thinking in short time spans of three to six months to thinking in strategic time spans of one to five years.

This longer-term planning allowed Spungin to develop a set of long-term goals and priorities. Soon, she took control of her own development. For example, it became clear to Spungin that corporate banking—which her colleagues believed to be her area of expertise based on her past experience—did not hold any real interest for her, even though she had accepted one banking project after another. Instead, she decided to shift her focus to the organizational practice, something she really enjoyed. (McKinsey, like many companies, allows its consultants significant flexibility in terms of choosing assignments, but most managers do not avail themselves of this opportunity.) By claiming a personal agenda and integrating short-, medium-, and long-term responsibilities into her broader master plan, Spungin felt much more motivated and excited about her work than she had when she was merely responding to everyday demands.

Finally, Spungin took charge of her time. She realized that trying to be accessible to everyone made her inaccessible to those who really needed her. She began prioritizing the time she spent with clients and team members. With her personal assistant's help, she streamlined her work. Previously, her assistant would schedule meetings in an ad hoc manner. Now, Spungin drove the calendar, so she could make the calls about which meetings she needed to attend. She began to recognize patterns of work intensity according to the time of year; for example, she travelled less in the fall, so Spungin set aside half a day each week to work on her long-term projects then. In the end, Spungin realized the irony of effective management: To quickly achieve the goals that mattered, she had to slow down and take control. To her surprise, the people who reported to her, as well as her supervisors and clients, responded well to her saying no.

Spungin was better able to respond to and shape the demands she chose to meet once she stopped trying to please everyone. She became more proactive—presenting her own goals and ideas to influence what others expected of her. By focusing on the most important demands, she exceeded expectations. One year after having been rated second from the bottom in her peer group, she scored second from the top. In June 2003, Spungin was named a McKinsey partner.

Developing Resources

In addition to lack of time, many managers complain about a shortage of people, money, and equipment, and a surplus of rules and regulations. They struggle with limited resources. While some feel frustrated and keep beating their heads against a wall to no avail, others just give up. Managers who develop a long-term strategy and attack their goals slowly, steadily, and strategically, on the other hand, can eventually win the backing they want.

Thomas Sattelberger faced all kinds of impossible constraints in 1994 when he left Daimler-Benz to join Lufthansa as the head of corporate management and human resources development. At the time, Lufthansa was in the middle of a strategic cost-savings program that required every unit to reduce its total expenditures by 4% each year for the next five years. Employees generally interpreted the cost-cutting directive to mean that investing in anything other than what was necessary to keep the lights on was verboten. Additionally, Lufthansa's HR processes were a mess; responses to routine requests often took months, and contracts frequently contained typographical errors. These kinds of operational problems had existed in the department for years.

For most managers in Sattelberger's position, the goals would have been simple: Get the HR department to a functional level without increasing costs, make sure it doesn't backslide, and collect a paycheck. But Sattelberger had much higher aspirations. He had come to Lufthansa with the dream of building Germany's most progressive corporate human resources organization, which would help transform the formerly state-operated company into a world-class airline. Specifically, he envisioned starting Germany's first corporate university, the Lufthansa School of Business, which would extend far beyond traditional approaches to training and development. The university would tighten the links between strategy and organizational and individual development. Its curricula, including master's and nondegree management programs, would be designed, run, and evaluated by academics and leaders from global companies, so Lufthansa's managers would learn from the best.

In pursuing his dream, Sattelberger chose a methodical, clever, and patient mode of attack. First, he created an imaginary blueprint depicting his university as a kind of leadership development temple. The architectural conceit—the temple being built brick by brick and pillar by pillar—helped Sattelberger develop a long-term, strategic implementation plan. Cleaning up basic HR processes, he reasoned, was analogous to laying the foundation. With that accomplished, he would erect a series of development programs, each acting as a pillar that would hold up the "roof" of Lufthansa's overall corporate strategy. Seeing his plan as a blueprint also helped Sattelberger separate the "must-haves" from the "nice-to-haves" and the "can-live-withouts," which enabled him to focus on only the most vital and achievable elements.

Sattelberger understood that he had to be flexible and that building his temple would demand years of methodical work. He never spoke about his vision as a whole because its overall cost would have frightened most of the stakeholders. Instead, he secured their commitment for individual projects and programs and implemented the initiatives sequentially.

Step two was to lay the foundation that he had imagined. Over the course of two years, Sattelberger reorganized HR processes so that requests were met in a timely matter and operations made more efficient. Given the dismal state of Lufthansa's HR systems, no one anticipated that Sattelberger could possibly meet, much less exceed, expectations. He showed them wrong.

Capitalizing on his new credibility, he next set to work on step three: building the individual pillars. One project, Explorer 21, was a comprehensive development initiative in which managers would learn from one another. A separate program, ProTeam, was designed for management trainees. And another large-scale program focused on emulating best practices from companies such as General Electric, Citibank, Deutsche Bank, Daimler-Benz, and SAS.

The spending cap was a significant hurdle. Sattelberger had persuaded top management to allow him to rent out some training rooms to other companies to raise money for these projects, but he needed more. He understood that there was a limit to how far and how fast he could push: If he pressed too hard, a backlash would ensue. So in petitioning for funds, Sattelberger made sure he was better prepared than his counterparts with arguments and facts. When the controller failed to give him the green light, he made his case directly to Jürgen Weber, the CEO. Weber agreed in principle that the corporate university project was worthwhile, although the conversation was not an easy one. "For God's sake, do it," he ended up telling Sattelberger, "but do it right and stick to your budget."

Weber and the board eventually began to see how Sattelberger's development programs fit together. Then, in March 1998—when he learned that Daimler-Benz was about to beat Lufthansa to the punch with a corporate university of its own—Sattelberger made his final move. Determined not to let Daimler prevail, he wrote a memo requesting the creation of the Lufthansa School of Business to the board of directors. It approved the request without a moment's hesitation or debate, and Lufthansa opened Europe's first corporate university the following month.

The whole process took time, something purposeful managers, as we have shown previously, claim for themselves. Sattelberger coped with many setbacks and accepted significant delays and even cancellations of different aspects of his initiative. He delayed his plans for the corporate university for the first two years so he could focus solely on putting HR in order. Then, slowly and progressively, he worked to relax resource constraints. Although he started with much less than he expected, he never allowed his resolve to wither. Lufthansa has never measured the precise payback from its school of business, but the subjective judgment of top management is that the return has been much higher than the investment.

Exploiting Alternatives

When it comes to making decisions or pursuing initiatives, managers also fall victim to the trap of unexplored choices. Specifically, they either do not recognize that they have choices or do not take advantage of those they know they have. Because managers ignore their freedom to act, they surrender their options. Purposeful initiators, by contrast, hone their personal expertise, which confers confidence, a wide perspective of a particular arena, and greater credibility. These managers develop the ability to see, grasp, and fight for opportunities as they arise.

Dan Andersson was a midlevel manager who worked for the oil-refining company ConocoPhillips in Stockholm. As a native of Finland, he brought to Conoco a precious managerial commodity: deep knowledge of the Finnish market. This knowledge enabled him to convey information about specific regional conditions to senior managers, who did not speak the language or understand Finland's business issues. Because he had been mentored by the managing director of Conoco's Nordic operations, Andersson quickly grasped how the managerial invisibles—informal rules and norms, decision-making processes, interpersonal relationships, and social dynamics—influenced the reception of new ideas. He intuitively sensed the right way to present a proposal and the extent to which he could push at a particular point of time.

Andersson was assigned to a team charged with exploring Conoco's possible entrance into the Finnish market, which involved breaking a 50-year monopoly in the region. The first task was to set up storage facilities in Finland, an estimated $1 million project that would allow Conoco to import its own petrol. After several months of intense searching, the team eventually found an existing tank terminal, located in the city of Turku, that Shell had abandoned decades previously. Built in the 1920s, the old tanks appeared to be clean and usable. The Conoco team thought the solution had been found. In the back of his mind, however, Andersson was already at work on contingency plans. Plan B was to build a new facility, plan C was to create a joint venture with a competitor, and plan D was to find an investor for the tanks.

After months of negotiation, Turku's officials approved Conoco's lease of the old tanks. Then came the fateful phone call from Conoco's laboratory: There was too much carbon in the steel; the tanks were unsuitable for storing petrol. Without its own storage facility, Conoco could not enter the Finnish market. There was no other facility in the country that Conoco could buy. Abandoning the project seemed the only choice. Everyone on the team gave up except Andersson, who proposed putting plan B into action.

With the support of the local authorities, he persuaded the Conoco senior team to visit Finland for face-to-face discussions about the possibility of Conoco building its own tanks at the site. Once Andersson's boss saw the land and sensed the opportunity, he grew enthusiastic about a ground-up approach. As it happened, however, the land was contaminated; cleanup would have cost tens of millions of euros. Still, Andersson persisted. Working with city officials, he discovered the original contracts clearly showed that Shell was responsible for the cleanup of the land. Once the cleanup was complete, Conoco began work on the new tanks. When the first Conoco ship arrived at the harbor, three years after the project had begun, city representatives, hundreds of spectators, Finnish television crews, and Conoco's top management were present to celebrate. Today, Conoco is the most efficient operator of automated self-service filling stations in Finland.

As a manager, Andersson's allegiance was not merely to a job but to accomplishing, one way or another, the strategic goals of his company. By scanning the environment for possible obstacles and searching for ways around them, he was able to expand his company's, and his own, scope of opportunity. Today, he is responsible for ConocoPhillips' retail development in Europe.

A bias for action is not a special gift of a few. Most managers can develop this capacity. Spungin's story demonstrates how focusing on a clear, long-term goal widened her horizon. Sattelberger and Andersson countered limitations with plans of their own and showed their companies what was possible.

In our studies of managers, we have found that the difference between those who take the initiative and those who do not becomes particularly evident during phases of major change, when managerial work becomes relatively chaotic and unstructured. Managers who fret about conforming to the explicit or imagined expectations of others respond to lack of structure by becoming disoriented and paralyzed. Effective managers, by contrast, seize the opportunity to extend the scope of their jobs, expand their choices, and pursue ambitious goals.

Once managers command their agendas and sense their own freedom of choice, they come to relish their roles. They begin to search for situations that go beyond their scope and enjoy seizing opportunities as they arise. Above all, effective managers with a bias for action aren't managed by their jobs; rather, the reverse is true.

Originally published in March 2004. Reprint R0403B

Note

1. The framework of demands, constraints, and choices as a way to think about managerial jobs was first suggested by Rosemary Stewart in her book *Managers and Their Jobs* (Macmillan, 1967). See also Rosemary Stewart, *Choices for the Manager* (Prentice Hall, 1982).

Moments of Greatness

by Robert E. Quinn

AS LEADERS, SOMETIMES we're truly "on," and sometimes we're not. Why is that? What separates the episodes of excellence from those of mere competence? In striving to tip the balance toward excellence, we try to identify great leaders' qualities and behaviors so we can develop them ourselves. Nearly all corporate training programs and books on leadership are grounded in the assumption that we should study the behaviors of those who have been successful and teach people to emulate them.

But my colleagues and I have found that when leaders do their best work, they don't copy anyone. Instead, they draw on their own fundamental values and capabilities—operating in a frame of mind that is true to them yet, paradoxically, not their normal state of being. I call it the *fundamental state of leadership*. It's the way we lead when we encounter a crisis and finally choose to move forward. Think back to a time when you faced a significant life challenge: a promotion opportunity, the risk of professional failure, a serious illness, a divorce, the death of a loved one, or any other major jolt. Most likely, if you made decisions not to meet others' expectations but to suit what you instinctively understood to be right—in other words, if you were at your very best—you rose to the task because you were being tested.

Is it possible to enter the fundamental state of leadership without crisis? In my work coaching business executives, I've found that if we ask ourselves—and honestly answer—just four questions, we can make the shift at any time. It's a temporary state. Fatigue and external resistance pull us out of it. But each time we reach it, we return to our everyday selves a bit more capable, and we usually elevate the performance of the people around us as well. Over time, we all can become more effective leaders by deliberately choosing to enter the fundamental state of leadership rather than waiting for crisis to force us there.

Defining the Fundamental State

Even those who are widely admired for their seemingly easy and natural leadership skills—presidents, prime ministers, CEOs—do not usually function in the fundamental state of leadership. Most of the time, they are in their normal state—a healthy and even necessary condition under many circumstances, but not one that's conducive to coping with crisis. In the normal state, people tend to stay within their comfort zones and allow external forces to direct their behaviors and decisions. They lose moral influence and often rely on rational argument and the exercise of authority to bring about change. Others comply with what these leaders ask, out of fear, but the result is usually unimaginative and incremental—and largely reproduces what already exists.

To elevate the performance of others, we must elevate ourselves into the fundamental state of leadership. Getting there requires a shift along four dimensions. (See the exhibit "There's Normal, and There's Fundamental.")

First, we move from being comfort centered to being results centered. The former feels safe but eventually leads to a sense of languishing and meaninglessness. In his book *The Path of Least Resistance,* Robert Fritz carefully explains how asking a single question can move us from the normal, reactive state to a much more generative condition. That question is this: What result do I want to

Idea in Brief

Like all leaders, sometimes you're "on," and sometimes you're not. How to tip the scale toward excellence and away from mere competence? Don't rely on imitating other leaders or poring over leadership manuals. Instead, enter the **fundamental state of leadership**: the way you lead when a crisis forces you to tap into your deepest values and instincts. In this state, you instinctively know what to do: You rise to the occasion and perform at your best.

Fortunately, you don't need a crisis to shift into the fundamental state of leadership. You can do so any time (before a crucial conversation, during a key meeting) by asking four questions:

- **"Am I results centered?"** Have you articulated the result you want to create?

- **"Am I internally directed?"** Are you willing to challenge others' expectations?

- **"Am I other focused?"** Have you put your organization's needs above your own?

- **"Am I externally open?"** Do you recognize signals suggesting the need for change?

No one can operate at the top of their game 24/7. But each time you enter the fundamental state of leadership, you make it easier to return to that state again. And you inspire others around you to higher levels of excellence.

create? Giving an honest answer pushes us off nature's path of least resistance. It leads us from problem solving to purpose finding.

Second, we move from being externally directed to being more internally directed. That means that we stop merely complying with others' expectations and conforming to the current culture. To become more internally directed is to clarify our core values and increase our integrity, confidence, and authenticity. As we become more confident and more authentic, we behave differently. Others must make sense of our new behavior. Some will be attracted to it, and some will be offended by it. That's not prohibitive, though: When we are true to our values, we are willing to initiate such conflict.

Third, we become less self-focused and more focused on others. We put the needs of the organization as a whole above our own. Few among us would admit that personal needs trump the collective

Idea in Practice

To enter the fundamental state of leadership, apply these steps:

1. **Recognize you've already been there.** You've faced great challenges before and, in surmounting them, you entered the fundamental state. By recalling these moments' lessons, you release positive emotions and see new possibilities for your current situation.

2. **Analyze your current state.** Compare your normal performance with what you've done at your very best. You'll fuel a desire to elevate what you're doing now and instill confidence that you can reenter the fundamental state.

3. **Ask the four questions shown in the following chart.**

BY ASKING . . .	YOU SHIFT FROM . . .	TO . . .
Am I results centered?	Remaining in your comfort zone and solving familiar problems	Moving toward possibilities that don't yet exist
Am I internally directed?	Complying with others' expectations and conforming to existing conditions	Clarifying your core values, acting with authenticity and confidence, and willingly initiating productive conflict
Am I other focused?	Allowing pursuit of your own self-interest to shape your relationships	Committing to the collective good in your organization—even at personal cost

good, but the impulse to control relationships in a way that feeds our own interests is natural and normal. That said, self-focus over time leads to feelings of isolation. When we put the collective good first, others reward us with their trust and respect. We form tighter, more sensitive bonds. Empathy increases, and cohesion follows. We create an enriched sense of community, and that helps us transcend the conflicts that are a necessary element in high-performing organizations.

Am I externally open?	Controlling your environment, making incremental changes, and relying on established routines	Learning from your environment, acknowledging the need for major change, and departing from routines

Example: John Jones, a successful change leader, had turned around two struggling divisions in his corporation. Promised the presidency of the largest division when the incumbent retired, he was told meanwhile to bide his time overseeing a dying division's "funeral." He determined to turn the division around. After nine months, though, he'd seen little improvement. Employees weren't engaged.

To enter the fundamental state, John asked:

- **"Am I results oriented?"** He suddenly envisioned a new strategy for his struggling division, along with a plan (including staff reassignments) for implementing it. With a clear, compelling strategy in mind, his energy soared.

- **"Am I internally directed?"** He realized that his focus on the promised plum job had prevented him from doing the hard work needed to motivate his division's people to give more.

- **"Am I other focused?"** He decided to turn down the presidency in favor of rescuing his failing division—a course truer to his leadership values. He thus traded personal security for a greater good.

- **"Am I externally open?"** He stopped deceiving himself into thinking he'd done all he could for his failing division and realized he had the capacity to improve things.

Fourth, we become more open to outside signals or stimuli, including those that require us to do things we are not comfortable doing. In the normal state, we pay attention to signals that we know to be relevant. If they suggest incremental adjustments, we respond. If, however, they call for more dramatic changes, we may adopt a posture of defensiveness and denial; this mode of self-protection and self-deception separates us from the ever-changing external world. We live according to an outdated, less valid, image of what is

There's normal, and there's fundamental

Under everyday circumstances, leaders can remain in their normal state of being and do what they need to do. But some challenges require a heightened perspective—what can be called the fundamental state of leadership. Here's how the two states differ.

In the normal state, I am . . .	In the fundamental state, I am . . .
COMFORT CENTERED	**RESULTS CENTERED**
I stick with what I know.	I venture beyond familiar territory to pursue ambitious new outcomes.
EXTERNALLY DIRECTED	**INTERNALLY DIRECTED**
I comply with others' wishes in an effort to keep the peace.	I behave according to my values.
SELF-FOCUSED	**OTHER FOCUSED**
I place my interests above those of the group.	I put the collective good first.
INTERNALLY CLOSED	**EXTERNALLY OPEN**
I block out external stimuli in order to stay on task and avoid risk.	I learn from my environment and recognize when there's a need for change.

real. But in the fundamental state of leadership, we are more aware of what is unfolding, and we generate new images all the time. We are adaptive, credible, and unique. In this externally open state, no two people are alike.

These four qualities—being results centered, internally directed, other focused, and externally open—are at the heart of positive human influence, which is generative and attractive. A person without these four characteristics can also be highly influential, but his or her influence tends to be predicated on some form of control or force, which does not usually give rise to committed followers. By entering the fundamental state of leadership, we increase the likelihood of attracting others to an elevated level of community, a high-performance state that may continue even when we are not present.

Preparing for the Fundamental State

Because people usually do not leave their comfort zones unless forced, many find it helpful to follow a process when they choose to enter the fundamental state of leadership. I teach a technique to executives and use it in my own work. It simply involves asking four awareness-raising questions designed to help us transcend our natural denial mechanisms. When people become aware of their hypocrisies, they are more likely to change. Those who are new to the "fundamental state" concept, however, need to take two preliminary steps before they can understand and employ it.

Step 1: Recognize that you have previously entered the fundamental state of leadership

Every reader of this publication has reached, at one time or another, the fundamental state of leadership. We've all faced a great personal or professional challenge and spent time in the dark night of the soul. In successfully working through such episodes, we inevitably enter the fundamental state of leadership.

When I introduce people to this concept, I ask them to identify two demanding experiences from their past and ponder what happened in terms of intention, integrity, trust, and adaptability. At first, they resist the exercise because I am asking them to revisit times of great personal pain. But as they recount their experiences, they begin to see that they are also returning to moments of greatness. Our painful experiences often bring out our best selves. Recalling the lessons of such moments releases positive emotions and makes it easier to see what's possible in the present. In this exercise, I ask people to consider their behavior during these episodes in relation to the characteristics of the fundamental state of leadership. (See the exhibit "You've Already Been There" for analyses of two actual episodes.)

Sometimes I also ask workshop participants to share their stories with one another. Naturally, they are reluctant to talk about such dark moments. To help people open up, I share my own moments of great challenge, the ones I would normally keep to myself. By exhibiting

You've already been there

Two participants in a leadership workshop at the University of Michigan's Ross School of Business used this self-assessment tool to figure out how they've transcended their greatest life challenges by entering the fundamental state of leadership. You can use the same approach in analyzing how you've conquered your most significant challenges.

	PARTICIPANT A	PARTICIPANT B
The pivotal crisis:	I was thrust into a job that was crucial to the organization but greatly exceeded my capabilities. I had to get people to do things they did not want to do.	I was driving myself hard at work, and things kept getting worse at home. Finally my wife told me she wanted a divorce.
How did you become more results centered?	I kept trying to escape doing what was required, but I could not stand the guilt. I finally decided I had to change. I envisioned what success might look like, and I committed to making whatever changes were necessary.	I felt I'd lost everything: family, wealth, and stature. I withdrew from relationships. I started drinking heavily. I finally sought professional help for my sorrow and, with guidance, clarified my values and made choices about my future.
How did you become more internally directed?	I stopped worrying so much about how other people would evaluate and judge me. I was starting to operate from my own values. I felt more self-empowered than ever and realized how fear driven I had been.	I engaged in a lot of self-reflection and journal writing. It became clear that I was not defined by marriage, wealth, or stature. I was more than that. I began to focus on how I could make a difference for other people. I got more involved in my community.
How did you become more focused on others?	I realized how much I needed people, and I became more concerned about them. I was better able to hear what they were saying. I talked not just from my head but also from my heart. My colleagues responded. Today, I am still close to those people.	As I started to grow and feel more self-confident, I became better at relating. At work, I now ask more of people than I ever did before, but I also give them far more support. I care about them, and they can tell.
How did you becom more externally open?	I experimented with new approaches. They often did not work, but they kept the brainstorming in motion. I paid attention to every kind of feedback. I was hungry to get it right. There was a lot of discovery. Each step forward was exhilarating.	I began to feel stronger. I was less intimidated when people gave me negative feedback. I think it was because I was less afraid of changing and growing.

vulnerability, I'm able to win the group's trust and embolden other people to exercise the same courage. I recently ran a workshop with a cynical group of executives. After I broke the testimonial ice, one of the participants told us of a time when he had accepted a new job that required him to relocate his family. Just before he was to start, his new boss called in a panic, asking him to cut his vacation short and begin work immediately. The entire New England engineering team had quit; clients in the region had no support whatsoever. The executive started his job early, and his family had to navigate the move without his help. He described the next few months as "the worst and best experience" of his life.

Another executive shared that he'd found out he had cancer the same week he was promoted and relocated to Paris, not knowing how to speak French. His voice cracked as he recalled these stressful events. But then he told us about the good that came out of them—how he conquered both the disease and the job while also becoming a more authentic and influential leader.

Others came forward with their own stories, and I saw a great change in the group. The initial resistance and cynicism began to disappear, and participants started exploring the fundamental state of leadership in a serious way. They saw the power in the concept and recognized that hiding behind their pride or reputation would only get in the way of future progress. In recounting their experiences, they came to realize that they had become more purposive, authentic, compassionate, and responsive.

Step 2: Analyze your current state

When we're in the fundamental state, we take on various positive characteristics, such as clarity of vision, self-empowerment, empathy, and creative thinking. (See the exhibit "Are You in the Fundamental State of Leadership?" for a checklist organized along the four dimensions.) Most of us would like to say we display these characteristics at all times, but we really do so only sporadically.

Comparing our normal performance with what we have done at our very best often creates a desire to elevate what we are doing now. Knowing we've operated at a higher level in the past instills

Are you in the fundamental state of leadership?

Think of a time when you reached the fundamental state of leadership—that is, when you were at your best as a leader—and use this checklist to identify the qualities you displayed. Then check off the items that describe your behavior today. Compare the past and present. If there's a significant difference, what changes do you need to make to get back to the fundamental state?

At my best I was ...	Today I am ...	
		RESULTS CENTERED
——	——	Knowing what result I'd like to create
——	——	Holding high standards
——	——	Initiating actions
——	——	Challenging people
——	——	Disrupting the status quo
——	——	Capturing people's attention
——	——	Feeling a sense of shared purpose
——	——	Engaging in urgent conversations
		INTERNALLY DIRECTED
——	——	Operating from my core values
——	——	Finding motivation from within
——	——	Feeling self-empowered
——	——	Leading courageously
——	——	Bringing hidden conflicts to the surface
——	——	Expressing what I really believe
——	——	Feeling a sense of shared reality
——	——	Engaging in authentic conversations
		OTHER FOCUSED
——	——	Sacrificing personal interests for the common good
——	——	Seeing the potential in everyone
——	——	Trusting others and fostering interdependence
——	——	Empathizing with people's needs
——	——	Expressing concern
——	——	Supporting people
——	——	Feeling a sense of shared identity
——	——	Engaging in participative conversations

		EXTERNALLY OPEN
___	___	Moving forward into uncertainty
___	___	Inviting feedback
___	___	Paying deep attention to what's unfolding
___	___	Learning exponentially
___	___	Watching for new opportunities
___	___	Growing continually
___	___	Feeling a sense of shared contribution
___	___	Engaging in creative conversations

confidence that we can do so again; it quells our fear of stepping into unknown and risky territory.

Asking Four Transformative Questions

Of course, understanding the fundamental state of leadership and recognizing its power are not the same as being there. Entering that state is where the real work comes in. To get started, we can ask ourselves four questions that correspond with the four qualities of the fundamental state.

To show how each of these qualities affects our behavior while we're in the fundamental state of leadership, I'll draw on stories from two executives. One is a company president; we'll call him John Jones. The other, Robert Yamamoto, is the executive director of the Los Angeles Junior Chamber of Commerce. Both once struggled with major challenges that changed the way they thought about their jobs and their lives.

I met John in an executive course I was teaching. He was a successful change leader who had turned around two companies in his corporation. Yet he was frustrated. He had been promised he'd become president of the largest company in the corporation as soon as the current president retired, which would happen in the near future. In the meantime, he had been told to bide his time with a company that everyone considered dead. His assignment was simply to oversee the funeral, yet he took it as a personal challenge to turn the company around. After he had been there nine months, however, there was little improvement, and the people were still not very engaged.

As for Robert, he had been getting what he considered to be acceptable (if not exceptional) results in his company. So when the new board president asked him to prepare a letter of resignation, Robert was stunned. He underwent a period of anguished introspection, during which he began to distrust others and question his own management skills and leadership ability. Concerned for his family and his future, he started to seek another job and wrote the requested letter.

As you will see, however, even though things looked grim for both Robert and John, they were on the threshold of positive change.

Am I results centered?

Most of the time, we are comfort centered. We try to continue doing what we know how to do. We may think we are pursuing new outcomes, but if achieving them means leaving our comfort zones, we subtly—even unconsciously—find ways to avoid doing so. We typically advocate ambitious outcomes while designing our work for maximum administrative convenience, which allows us to avoid conflict but frequently ends up reproducing what already exists. Often, others collude with us to act out this deception. Being comfort centered is hypocritical, self-deceptive, and normal.

Clarifying the result we want to create requires us to reorganize our lives. Instead of moving away from a problem, we move toward a possibility that does not yet exist. We become more proactive, intentional, optimistic, invested, and persistent. We also tend to become more energized, and our impact on others becomes energizing.

Consider what happened with John. When I first spoke with him, he sketched out his strategy with little enthusiasm. Sensing that lack of passion, I asked him a question designed to test his commitment to the end he claimed he wanted to obtain:

> What if you told your people the truth? Suppose you told
> them that nobody really expects you to succeed, that you
> were assigned to be a caretaker for 18 months, and that you

have been promised a plum job once your assignment is through. And then you tell them that you have chosen instead to give up that plum job and bet your career on the people present. Then, from your newly acquired stance of optimism for the company's prospects, you issue some challenges beyond your employees' normal capacity.

To my surprise, John responded that he was beginning to think along similar lines. He grabbed a napkin and rapidly sketched out a new strategy along with a plan for carrying it out, including reassignments for his staff. It was clear and compelling, and he was suddenly full of energy.

What happened here? John was the president of his company and therefore had authority. And he'd turned around two other companies—evidence that he had the knowledge and competencies of a change leader. Yet he was *failing* as a change leader. That's because he had slipped into his comfort zone. He was going through the motions, doing what had worked elsewhere. He was imitating a great leader—in this case, John himself. But imitation is not the way to enter the fundamental state of leadership. If I had accused John of not being committed to a real vision, he would have been incensed. He would have argued heatedly in denial of the truth. All I had to do, though, was nudge him in the right direction. As soon as he envisioned the result he wanted to create and committed himself to it, a new strategy emerged and he was reenergized.

Then there was Robert, who went to what he assumed would be his last board meeting and found that he had more support than he'd been led to believe. Shockingly, at the end of the meeting, he still had his job. Even so, this fortuitous turn brought on further soul-searching. Robert started to pay more attention to what he was doing; he began to see his tendency to be tactical and to gravitate toward routine tasks. He concluded that he was managing, not leading. He was playing a role and abdicating leadership to the board president—not because that person had the knowledge and vision to lead but because the position came with the statutory right to lead.

"I suddenly decided to really lead my organization," Robert said. "It was as if a new person emerged. The decision was not about me. I needed to do it for the good of the organization."

In deciding to "really lead," Robert started identifying the strategic outcomes he wanted to create. As he did this, he found himself leaving his zone of comfort—behaving in new ways and generating new outcomes.

Am I internally directed?

In the normal state, we comply with social pressures in order to avoid conflict and remain connected with our coworkers. However, we end up feeling *less* connected because conflict avoidance results in political compromise. We begin to lose our uniqueness and our sense of integrity. The agenda gradually shifts from creating an external result to preserving political peace. As this problem intensifies, we begin to lose hope and energy.

This loss was readily apparent in the case of John. He was his corporation's shining star. But since he was at least partially focused on the future reward—the plum job—he was not fully focused on doing the hard work he needed to do at the moment. So he didn't ask enough of the people he was leading. To get more from them, John needed to be more internally directed.

Am I other focused?

It's hard to admit, but most of us, most of the time, put our own needs above those of the whole. Indeed, it is healthy to do so; it's a survival mechanism. But when the pursuit of our own interests controls our relationships, we erode others' trust in us. Although people may comply with our wishes, they no longer derive energy from their relationships with us. Over time we drive away the very social support we seek.

To become more focused on others is to commit to the collective good in relationships, groups, or organizations, even if it means incurring personal costs. When John made the shift into the fundamental state of leadership, he committed to an uncertain future for himself. He had been promised a coveted job. All he had to do was wait a few months. Still, he was unhappy, so he chose to turn down the opportunity in favor of a course that was truer to his leadership values. When he shifted gears, he sacrificed his personal security in favor of a greater good.

Remember Robert's words: "The decision was not about me. I needed to do it for the good of the organization." After entering the fundamental state of leadership, he proposed a new strategic direction to the board's president and said that if the board didn't like it, he would walk away with no regrets. He knew that the strategy would benefit the organization, regardless of how it would affect him personally. Robert put the good of the organization first. When a leader does this, people notice, and the leader gains respect and trust. Group members, in turn, become more likely to put the collective good first. When they do, tasks that previously seemed impossible become doable.

Am I externally open?

Being closed to external stimuli has the benefit of keeping us on task, but it also allows us to ignore signals that suggest a need for change. Such signals would force us to cede control and face risk, so denying them is self-protective, but it is also self-deceptive. John convinced himself he'd done all he could for his failing company when, deep down, he knew that he had the capacity to improve things. Robert was self-deceptive, too, until crisis and renewed opportunity caused him to open up and explore the fact that he was playing a role accorded him but not using his knowledge and emotional capacity to transcend that role and truly lead his people.

Asking ourselves whether we're externally open shifts our focus from controlling our environment to learning from it and helps us recognize the need for change. Two things happen as a result. First, we are forced to improvise in response to previously unrecognized cues—that is, to depart from established routines. And second, because trial-and-error survival requires an accurate picture of the results we're creating, we actively and genuinely seek honest feedback. Since people trust us more when we're in this state, they tend to offer more accurate feedback, understanding that we are likely to learn from the message rather than kill the messenger.

A cycle of learning and empowerment is created, allowing us to see things that people normally cannot see and to formulate transformational strategies.

Applying the Fundamental Principles

Just as I teach others about the fundamental state of leadership, I also try to apply the concept in my own life. I was a team leader on a project for the University of Michigan's Executive Education Center. Usually, the center runs weeklong courses that bring in 30 to 40 executives. It was proposed that we develop a new product, an integrated week of perspectives on leadership. C. K. Prahalad would begin with a strategic perspective, then Noel Tichy, Dave Ulrich, Karl Weick, and I would follow with our own presentations. The objective was to fill a 400-seat auditorium. Since each presenter had a reasonably large following in some domain of the executive world, we were confident we could fill the seats, so we scheduled the program for the month of July, when our facilities were typically underutilized.

In the early months of planning and organizing, everything went perfectly. A marketing consultant had said we could expect to secure half our enrollment three weeks prior to the event. When that time rolled around, slightly less than half of the target audience had signed up, so we thought all was well. But then a different consultant indicated that for our kind of event we would get few additional enrollments during the last three weeks. This stunning prediction meant that attendance would be half of what we expected and we would be lucky to break even.

As the team leader, I could envision the fallout. Our faculty members, accustomed to drawing a full house, would be offended by a half-empty room; the dean would want to know what went wrong; and the center's staff would probably point to the team leader as the problem. That night I spent several hours pacing the floor. I was filled with dread and shame. Finally I told myself that this kind of behavior was useless. I went to my desk and wrote down the four questions. As I considered them, I concluded that I was comfort centered, externally directed, self-focused, and internally closed.

So I asked myself, "What result do I want to create?" I wrote that I wanted the center to learn how to offer a new, world-class product that would be in demand over time. With that clarification came a freeing insight: Because this was our first offering of the product, turning a large profit was not essential. That would be nice, of course, but we'd be happy to learn how to do such an event properly, break even, and lay the groundwork for making a profit in the future.

I then asked myself, "How can I become other focused?" At that moment, I was totally self-focused—I was worried about my reputation—and my first inclination was to be angry with the staff. But in shifting my focus to what they might be thinking that night, I realized they were most likely worried that I'd come to work in the morning ready to assign blame. Suddenly, I saw a need to both challenge and support them.

Finally, I thought about how I could become externally open. It would mean moving forward and learning something new, even if that made me uncomfortable. I needed to engage in an exploratory dialogue rather than preside as the expert in charge.

I immediately began making a list of marketing strategies, though I expected many of them would prove foolish since I knew nothing about marketing. The next day, I brought the staff together—and they, naturally, were guarded. I asked them what result we wanted to create. What happened next is a good example of how contagious the fundamental state of leadership can be.

We talked about strategies for increasing attendance, and after a while, I told the staff that I had some silly marketing ideas and was embarrassed to share them but was willing to do anything to help. They laughed at many of my naive thoughts about how to increase publicity and create pricing incentives. Yet my proposals also sparked serious discussion, and the group began to brainstorm its way into a collective strategy. Because I was externally open, there was space and time for everyone to lead. People came up with better ways of approaching media outlets and creating incentives. In that meeting, the group developed a shared sense of purpose, reality, identity, and contribution. They left feeling reasonable optimism and went forward as a committed team.

In the end, we did not get 400 participants, but we filled more than enough seats to have a successful event. We more than broke even, and we developed the skills we needed to run such an event better in the future. The program was a success because something transformational occurred among the staff. Yet the transformation did not originate in the meeting. It began the night before, when I asked myself the four questions and moved from the normal, reactive state to the fundamental state of leadership. And my entry into the fundamental state encouraged the staff to enter as well.

While the fundamental state proves useful in times of crisis, it can also help us cope with more mundane challenges. If I am going to have an important conversation, attend a key meeting, participate in a significant event, or teach a class, part of my preparation is to try to reach the fundamental state of leadership. Whether I am working with an individual, a group, or an organization, I ask the same four questions. They often lead to high-performance outcomes, and the repetition of high-performance outcomes can eventually create a high-performance culture.

Inspiring Others to High Performance

When we enter the fundamental state of leadership, we immediately have new thoughts and engage in new behaviors. We can't remain in this state forever. It can last for hours, days, or sometimes months, but eventually we come back to our normal frame of mind. While the fundamental state is temporary, each time we are in it we learn more about people and our environment and increase the probability that we will be able to return to it. Moreover, we inspire those around us to higher levels of performance.

To this day, Robert marvels at the contrast between his organization's past and present. His transformation into a leader with positive energy and a willingness and ability to tackle challenges in new ways helped shape the L.A. Junior Chamber of Commerce into a high-functioning and creative enterprise. When I last spoke to Robert, here's what he had to say:

> I have a critical mass of individuals on both the staff and the board who are willing to look at our challenges in a new way and work on solutions together. At our meetings, new energy is present. What previously seemed unimaginable now seems to happen with ease.

Any CEO would be delighted to be able to say these things. But the truth is, it's not a typical situation. When Robert shifted into the fundamental state of leadership, his group (which started off in a normal state) came to life, infused with his renewed energy and vision. Even after he'd left the fundamental state, the group sustained a higher level of performance. It continues to flourish, without significant staff changes or restructuring.

All this didn't happen because Robert read a book or an article about the best practices of some great leader. It did not happen because he was imitating someone else. It happened because he was jolted out of his comfort zone and was forced to enter the fundamental state of leadership. He was driven to clarify the result he wanted to create, to act courageously from his core values, to surrender his self-interest to the collective good, and to open himself up to learning in real time. From Robert, and others like him, we can learn the value of challenging ourselves in this way—a painful process but one with great potential to make a positive impact on our own lives and on the people around us.

Originally published in July 2005. Reprint R0507F

What to Ask the Person in the Mirror

by Robert S. Kaplan

IF YOU'RE LIKE MOST successful leaders, you were, in the early stages of your career, given plenty of guidance and support. You were closely monitored, coached, and mentored. But as you moved up the ladder, the sources of honest and useful feedback became fewer, and after a certain point, you were pretty much on your own. Now, your boss—if you have one—is no longer giving much consideration to your day-to-day actions. By the time any mistakes come to light, it's probably too late to fix them—or your boss's perceptions of you. And by the time your management missteps negatively affect your business results, it's usually too late to make corrections that will get you back on course.

No matter how talented and successful you are, you will make mistakes. You will develop bad habits. The world will change subtly, without your even noticing, and behaviors that once worked will be rendered ineffective. Over a 22-year career at Goldman Sachs, I had the opportunity to run various businesses and to work with or coach numerous business leaders. I chaired the firm's senior leadership training efforts and cochaired its partnership committee, which focused on reviews, promotions, and development of managing directors. Through this experience and subsequent interviews with a large number of executives in a broad range of industries, I have observed that even outstanding leaders invariably struggle through stretches of their careers where they get off track for some period of time.

It's hard to see it when you're in the midst of it; changes in the environment, competitors, or even personal circumstances can quietly guide you off your game. I have learned that a key characteristic of highly successful leaders is not that they figure out how to always stay on course, but that they develop techniques to help them recognize a deteriorating situation and get back on track as quickly as possible. In my experience, the best way to do that is to step back regularly, say, every three to six months (and certainly whenever things feel as though they aren't going well), and honestly ask yourself some questions about how you're doing and what you may need to do differently. As simple as this process sounds, people are often shocked by their own answers to basic management and leadership questions.

One manager in a large financial services company who had been passed over for promotion told me he was quite surprised by his year-end performance review, which highlighted several management issues that had not been previously brought to his attention. His boss read several comments from the review that faulted him for poor communication, failure to effectively articulate a strategy for the business, and a tendency to isolate himself from his team. He believed that the review was unfair. After 15 years at the company, he began to feel confused and misunderstood and wondered whether he still had a future there. He decided to seek feedback directly from five of his key contributors and longtime collaborators. In one-on-one meetings, he asked them for blunt feedback and advice. He was shocked to hear that they were highly critical of several of his recent actions, were confused about the direction he wanted to take the business, and felt he no longer valued their input. Their feedback helped him see that he had been so immersed in the day-to-day business that he had failed to step back and think about what he was doing. This was a serious wake-up call. He immediately took steps to change his behavior and address these issues. His review the following year was dramatically better, he was finally promoted, and his business's performance improved. The manager was lucky to have received this feedback in time to get his career back on track, although he regretted that he had waited for a negative review to ask

Idea in Brief

If you're like most managers, the higher you go up the corporate ladder, the harder it is to get candid feedback on your performance. And without crucial input from bosses and colleagues, you can make mistakes that irreparably damage your organization—and your reputation.

How can you figure out how you're *really* doing and avoid business disasters? Kaplan recommends looking to *yourself* for answers. Regularly ask yourself questions like these: "Am I communicating a vision for my business to my employees?" "Am I spending my time in ways that enable me to achieve my priorities?" "Do I give people timely and direct feedback they can act on?" "How do I behave under pressure?"

It's far more important to ask the *right* questions than to have all the answers. By applying this process, you tackle the leadership challenges that inevitably arise during the course of your career—and craft new plans for staying on your game.

basic questions about his leadership activities. He promised himself he would not make that mistake again.

In this article, I outline seven types of questions that leaders should ask themselves on some periodic basis. I am not suggesting that there is a "right" answer to any of them or that they all will resonate with a given executive at any point in time. I am suggesting that successful executives can regularly improve their performance and preempt serious business problems by stepping back and taking the time to ask themselves certain key questions.

Vision and Priorities

It's surprising how often business leaders fail to ask themselves: *How frequently do I communicate a vision and priorities for my business? Would my employees, if asked, be able to articulate the vision and priorities?* Many leaders have, on paper, a wealth of leadership talents: interpersonal, strategic, and analytic skills; a knack for team building; and certainly the ability to develop a vision. Unfortunately, in the press of day-to-day activities, they often don't adequately communicate the vision to the organization, and in particular, they

Idea in Practice

Kaplan suggests periodically asking yourself questions related to seven leadership challenges.

To address this leadership challenge . . .	Ask . . .	Because . . .
Vision and priorities	How often do I communicate a vision and key priorities to achieve that vision?	Employees want to know where the business is going and what they need to focus on in order to help drive the business. As the world changes, they want to know how the vision and priorities might change.
Managing time	Does the way I spend my time match my key priorities?	Tracking your use of time can reveal startling—even horrifying—disconnects between your top priorities and your actions. Such disconnects send confusing messages to employees about your true priorities.
Feedback	Do I give people timely and direct feedback they can act on?	Employees want truthful, direct, and timely feedback. Retention and productivity improve when employees trust you to raise issues promptly and honestly.

don't convey it in a way that helps their people understand what they are supposed to be doing to drive the business. It is very difficult to lead people if they don't have a firm grasp of where they're heading and what's expected of them.

This was the problem at a large *Fortune* 200 company that had decided to invest in its 1,000 top managers by having them attend an intensive, two-day management-training program, 100 at a time. Before each session, the participants went through a 360-degree nonevaluative review in which critical elements of their individual performance were ranked by ten of their subordinates. The company's

Succession planning	Have I identified potential successors?	It's important to nurture future leaders who can grow the business. If you haven't identified possible successors, you're probably not delegating as much as you should, and you may even be a decision-making bottleneck.
Evaluation and alignment	Am I attuned to business changes that may require shifts in how we run the company?	All businesses encounter challenges posed by changes; for example, in customers' needs or the business's stage of maturity. To determine how best to evolve your business, regularly scan for changes, seek fresh perspectives from talented subordinates, and envision new organizational designs.
Leading under pressure	How do I behave under pressure?	During crises, employees watch you with a microscope—and mimic your behavior. By identifying your unproductive behaviors under pressure (such as blaming others or losing your temper), you can better manage those behaviors and avoid sending unintended messages to employees about how *they* should behave.
Staying true to yourself	Does my leadership style reflect who I truly am?	A business career is a marathon, not a sprint. If you've adopted a leadership style that doesn't suit your skills, values, and personality, you'll wear down.

senior management looked at the results, focusing on the top five and bottom five traits for each group. Despite this being an extremely well-managed firm, the ability to articulate a vision ranked in the bottom five for almost every group. Managers at that company did articulate a vision, but the feedback from their subordinates strongly indicated that they were not communicating it frequently or clearly enough to meet their people's tremendous hunger for guidance.

Employees want to know where the business is going and what they need to focus on. As the world changes, they want to know how the business vision and priorities might change along with it. While managers are taught to actively communicate, many either unintentionally undercommunicate or fail to articulate specific priorities that would give meaning to their vision. However often you think you discuss vision and strategy, you may not be doing it frequently enough or in sufficient detail to suit the needs of your people. Look at the CEO of an emerging biotechnology company, who was quite frustrated with what he saw as a lack of alignment within his top management team. He strongly believed that the company needed to do a substantial equity financing within the next 18 months, but his senior managers wanted to wait a few years until two or three of the company's key drugs were further along in the FDA approval process. They preferred to tell their story to investors when the company was closer to generating revenue. When I asked him about the vision for the company, the CEO sheepishly realized that he had never actually written down a vision statement. He had a well-articulated tactical plan relating to each of the company's specific product efforts but no fully formed vision that would give further context to these efforts. He decided to organize an off-site meeting for his senior management team to discuss and specifically articulate a vision for the company.

After a vigorous debate, the group quickly agreed on a vision and strategic priorities. They realized that in order to achieve their shared goals, the business would in fact require substantial financing sooner rather than later—or they would need to scale back some of the initiatives that were central to their vision for the company. Once they fully appreciated this trade-off, they understood what the CEO was trying to accomplish and left the meeting united about their financing strategy. The CEO was quite surprised at how easy it had been to bring the members of his leadership team together. Because they agreed on where they were going as a company, specific issues were much easier to resolve.

A common pitfall in articulating a vision is a failure to boil it down to a manageable list of initiatives. Culling the list involves thinking through and then making difficult choices and trade-off decisions. These choices communicate volumes to your people about how they should be spending their time. I spoke with the manager of a national sales force who felt frustrated that his direct reports were not focusing on the tasks necessary to achieve their respective regional sales goals. As a result, sales were growing at a slower rate than budgeted at the beginning of the year. When I asked him to enumerate the three to five key priorities he expected his salespeople to focus on, he paused and then explained that there were 15 and it would be very difficult to narrow the list down to five.

Even as he spoke, a light went on in his head. He realized why there might be a disconnect between him and his people: They didn't know precisely what he wanted because he had not told them in a prioritized, and therefore actionable, manner. He reflected on this issue for the next two weeks, thinking at length about his own experience as a regional manager and consulting with various colleagues. He then picked three priorities that he felt were crucial to achieving sales growth. The most important of these involved a major new-business targeting exercise followed by a substantial new-prospect calling effort. The regional managers immediately understood and began focusing on these initiatives. The fact is that having 15 priorities is the same as having none at all. Managers have a responsibility to translate their vision into a manageable number of priorities that their subordinates can understand and act on.

Failing to communicate your vision and priorities has direct costs to you in terms of time and business effectiveness. It's hard to delegate if your people don't have a good sense of the big picture; hence you end up doing more work yourself. This issue can cascade through the organization if your direct reports are, in turn, unable to communicate a vision and effectively leverage their own subordinates.

Managing Time

The second area to question is painfully simple and closely relates to the first: *How am I spending my time?* Once you know your priorities, you need to determine whether you're spending your time—your most precious asset—in a way that will allow you to achieve them. For example, if your two major priorities are senior talent development and global expansion but you're spending the majority of your

Testing Yourself

To assess your performance and stay on track, you should step back and ask yourself certain key questions.

Vision and Priorities

In the press of day-to-day activities, leaders often fail to adequately communicate their vision to the organization, and in particular, they don't communicate it in a way that helps their subordinates determine where to focus their own efforts.

How often do I communicate a vision for my business?

Have I identified and communicated three to five key priorities to achieve that vision?

If asked, would my employees be able to articulate the vision and priorities?

Managing Time

Leaders need to know how they're spending their time. They also need to ensure that their time allocation (and that of their subordinates) matches their key priorities.

How am I spending my time? Does it match my key priorities?

How are my subordinates spending their time? Does that match the key priorities for the business?

Feedback

Leaders often fail to coach employees in a direct and timely fashion and, instead, wait until the year-end review. This approach may lead to unpleasant surprises and can undermine effective professional development. Just as important, leaders need to cultivate subordinates who can give them advice and feedback during the year.

Do I give people timely and direct feedback that they can act on?

Do I have five or six junior subordinates who will tell me things I may not want to hear but need to hear?

Succession Planning

When leaders fail to actively plan for succession, they do not delegate sufficiently and may become decision-making bottlenecks. Key employees may leave if they are not actively groomed and challenged.

Have I, at least in my own mind, picked one or more potential successors?

Am I coaching them and giving them challenging assignments?

Am I delegating sufficiently? Have I become a decision-making bottleneck?

Evaluation and Alignment

The world is constantly changing, and leaders need to be able to adapt their businesses accordingly.

Is the design of my company still aligned with the key success factors for the business?

If I had to design my business with a clean sheet of paper, how would I design it? How would it differ from the current design?

Should I create a task force of subordinates to answer these questions and make recommendations to me?

Leading Under Pressure

A leader's actions in times of stress are watched closely by subordinates and have a profound impact on the culture of the firm and employees' behavior. Successful leaders need to be aware of their own stress triggers and consciously modulate their behavior during these periods to make sure they are acting in ways that are consistent with their beliefs and core values.

What types of events create pressure for me?

How do I behave under pressure?

What signals am I sending my subordinates? Are these signals helpful, or are they undermining the success of my business?

Staying True to Yourself

Successful executives develop leadership styles that fit the needs of their business but also fit their own beliefs and personality.

Is my leadership style comfortable? Does it reflect who I truly am?

Do I assert myself sufficiently, or have I become tentative?

Am I too politically correct?

Does worry about my next promotion or bonus cause me to pull punches or hesitate to express my views?

time on domestic operational and administrative matters that could be delegated, then you need to recognize there is a disconnect and you'd better make some changes.

It's such a simple question, yet many leaders, myself included, just can't accurately answer at times. When leaders finally do track their time, they're often surprised by what they find. Most of us go through periods where unexpected events and day-to-day chaos cause us to be reactive rather than acting on a proscribed plan. Crises, surprises, personnel issues, and interruptions make the workweek seem like a blur. I have recommended to many leaders that they track how they spend each hour of each day for one week, then categorize the hours into types of activities: business development, people management, and strategic planning, for example. For most executives, the results of this exercise are startling—even horrifying—with obvious disconnects between what their top priorities are and how they are spending their time.

For example, the CEO of a midsize manufacturing company was frustrated because he was working 70 hours a week and never seemed to catch up. His family life suffered, and, at work, he was constantly unavailable for his people and major customers. I suggested he step back and review how he was managing his time hour-by-hour over the course of a week. We sat down to examine the results and noticed that he was spending a substantial amount of time approving company expenditures, some for as little as $500—this in a business with $500 million in sales. Sitting in my office, he struggled to explain why he had not delegated some portion of this responsibility; it turned out that the activity was a holdover from a time when the company was much smaller. By delegating authority to approve recurring operating expenses below $25,000, he realized he could save as much as 15 hours per week. He was amazed that he had not recognized this issue and made this simple change much earlier.

How you spend your time is an important question not only for you but for your team. People tend to take their cues from the leader when it comes to time management—therefore, you want to make sure there's a match between your actions, your business priorities, and your team's activities. The CEO of a rapidly growing, 300-person professional services firm felt that, to build the business, senior managers needed to develop stronger and more substantive relationships with clients. This meant that senior professionals would need to spend significantly more time out of their offices in meetings with clients. When asked how his own time was being spent, the CEO was unable to answer. After tracking it for a week, he was shocked to find that he was devoting a tremendous amount of his time to administrative activities related to managing the firm. He realized that the amount of attention he was paying to these matters did not reflect the business's priorities and was sending a confusing message to his people. He immediately began pushing himself to delegate a number of these administrative tasks and increase the amount of time he spent on the road with customers, setting a powerful example for his people. He directed each of his senior managers to do a similar time-allocation exercise to ensure they were dedicating sufficient time to clients.

Of course, the way a leader spends his or her time must be tailored to the needs of the business, which may vary depending on time of year, personnel changes, and external factors. The key here is, whatever you decide, time allocation needs to be a conscious decision that fits your vision and priorities for the business. Given the pressure of running a business, it is easy to lose focus, so it's important to ask yourself this question periodically. Just as you would step back and review a major investment decision, you need to dispassionately review the manner in which you invest your time.

Feedback

When you think about the ways you approach feedback, you should first ask: *Do I give people timely, direct, and constructive feedback?* And second: *Do I have five or six junior people who will tell me things I don't want to hear but need to hear?*

If they're like most ambitious employees, your subordinates want to be coached and developed in a truthful and direct manner. They want to get feedback while there's still an opportunity to act on it; if you've waited until the year-end review, it's often too late. In my experience, well-intentioned managers typically fail to give blunt, direct, and timely feedback to their subordinates.

One reason for this failure is that managers are often afraid that constructive feedback and criticism will demoralize their employees. In addition, critiquing a professional in a frank and timely manner may be perceived as overly confrontational. Lastly, many managers fear that this type of feedback will cause employees not to like them. Consequently, leaders often wait until year-end performance reviews. The year-end review is evaluative (that is, the verdict on the year) and therefore is not conducive to constructive coaching. The subordinate is typically on the defensive and not as open to criticism. This approach creates surprises, often unpleasant ones, which undermine trust and dramatically reduce the confidence of the subordinate in the manager.

The reality is that managers who don't give immediate and direct feedback often are "liked" until year-end—at which time they wind up being strongly disliked. If employees have fallen short of expectations, the failing is reflected in bonuses, raises, and promotions. The feeling of injustice can be enormous. What's worse is the knowledge that if an employee had received feedback earlier in the year, it is likely that he or she would have made meaningful efforts to improve and address the issues.

While people do like to hear positive feedback, ultimately, they desperately want to know the truth, and I have rarely seen someone quit over hearing the truth or being challenged to do better—unless it's too late. On the contrary, I would argue that people are more likely to stay if they understand what issues they need to address and they trust you to bring those issues to their attention in a straightforward and prompt fashion. They gain confidence that you will work with them to develop their skills and that they won't be blindsided at the end of the year. Employees who don't land a hoped-for promotion will be much more likely to forgive you if you've told them all along what they need to do better, even if they haven't gotten there yet. They may well redouble their efforts to prove to you that they can overcome these issues.

During my career at Goldman Sachs, I consistently found that professional development was far more effective when coaching and direct feedback were given to employees throughout the year—well in advance of the annual performance review process. Internal surveys of managing directors showed that, in cases where feedback was confined to the year-end review, satisfaction with career development was dramatically lower than when it was offered throughout the year.

As hard as it is to give effective and timely feedback, many leaders find it much more challenging to get feedback from their employees. Once you reach a certain stage of your career, junior people are in a much better position than your boss to tell you how you're doing. They see you in your day-to-day activities, and they experience your decisions directly. Your boss, at this stage, is much more removed and, as a result, typically needs to talk to your subordinates to assess your performance at the end of the year. In order to avoid your own year-end surprises, you need to develop a network of junior professionals who are willing to give you constructive feedback. The problem is that, while your direct reports know what you are doing wrong, most of them are not dying to tell you. With good reason—there's very little upside and a tremendous amount of downside. The more senior and the more important you become, the less your subordinates will tell you the "awful truth"—things that are difficult to hear but that you need to know.

It takes a concerted effort to cultivate subordinates who will advise and coach you. It also takes patience and some relentlessness. When I ask subordinates for constructive feedback, they will typically and predictably tell me that I'm doing "very well." When I follow up and ask "What should I do differently?" they respond, "Nothing that I can think of." If I challenge them by saying, "There must be something!" still they say, "Nothing comes to mind." I then ask them to sit back and think—we have plenty of time. By this time, beads of sweat begin to become visible on their foreheads. After an awkward silence, they will eventually come up with something—and it's often devastating to hear. It's devastating because it's a damning criticism and because you know it's true.

What you do with this feedback is critical. If you act on it, you will improve your performance. Equally important, you will take a big step in building trust and laying the groundwork for a channel of honest feedback. When subordinates see that you respond positively to suggestions, they will often feel more ownership in the business and in your success. They'll learn to give you criticisms on their own initiative because they know you will actually appreciate it and do something with it. Developing a network of "coaching" subordinates will help you take action to identify your own leadership issues and meaningfully improve your performance.

Succession Planning

Another question that managers know is important yet struggle to answer affirmatively is: *Have I, at least in my own mind, picked one or more potential successors?* This issue is critical because if you aren't identifying potential successors, you are probably not delegating as extensively as you should and you may well be a decision-making bottleneck. Being a bottleneck invariably means that you are not spending enough time on vital leadership priorities and are failing to develop your key subordinates. Ironically, when leaders believe they are so talented that they can perform tasks far better than any of their subordinates and therefore insist on doing the tasks themselves, they will typically cause their businesses to underperform, and, ultimately, their careers will suffer as well.

The succession question also has significant implications that cascade through an organization: If leaders do not develop successors, then the organization may lack a sufficient number of leaders to successfully grow the business. Worse, if junior employees are not developed, they may leave the firm for better opportunities elsewhere. For these reasons, many well-managed companies will hesitate to promote executives who have failed to develop successors.

It is sufficient to identify possible successors without actually telling them you've done so—as long as this identification causes you to manage them differently. In particular, you will want to delegate more of your major responsibilities to these professionals. This will speed their maturation and prepare them to step up to the next level. By giving demanding assignments to these subordinates, you strongly signal an interest in their development and career progression—which will encourage them to turn down offers from competitors. Leaders who do this are much better able to keep their teams together and avoid losing up-and-coming stars to competitors.

A loss of talent is highly damaging to a company. It is particularly painful if you could have retained key employees by simply challenging them more intensively. I spoke with a division head of a large company who was concerned about what he perceived to be a talent deficit in his organization. He felt that he could not use his time to the fullest because he viewed his direct reports as incapable of assuming some of his major responsibilities. He believed this talent deficit was keeping him from launching several new product and market initiatives. In the midst of all this, he lost two essential subordinates over six months—each had left to take on increased responsibilities at major competitors. He had tried to persuade them to stay, emphasizing that he was actively considering them for significant new leadership assignments. Because they had not seen evidence of this previously, they were skeptical and left anyway. I asked him whether, prior to the defections, he had identified them (or anyone else) as potential successors, put increased responsibilities in their hands, or actively ratcheted up his coaching of these professionals. He answered that, in the chaos of daily events and in the effort to keep up with the business, he had not done so. He also admitted that he had underestimated the potential of these two employees and realized he was probably underestimating the abilities of several others in the company. He immediately sat down and made a list of potential stars and next to each name wrote out a career and responsibility game plan. He immediately got to work on this formative succession plan, although he suspected that he had probably waited too long already.

When you're challenging and testing people, you delegate to them more often, which frees you to focus on the most critical strategic matters facing the business. This will make you more successful and a more attractive candidate for your own future promotion.

Evaluation and Alignment

The world is constantly changing. Your customers' needs change; your business evolves (going, for instance, from high growth to mature); new products and distribution methods emerge as threats. When these changes happen, if you don't change along with them, you can get seriously out of alignment. The types of people you hire, the way you organize them, the economic incentives you offer them, and even the nature of the tasks you delegate no longer create the culture and outcomes that are critical to the success of your business. It's your job to make sure that the design of your organization is aligned with the key success factors for the business. Ask yourself: *Am I attuned to changes in the business environment that would require a change in the way we organize and run our business?*

Such clear-sightedness is, of course, hard to achieve. As a leader, you may be too close to the business to see subtle changes that are continually occurring. Because you probably played a central role in building and designing the business, it may be emotionally very difficult to make meaningful changes. You may have to fire certain employees—people you recruited and hired. You may also have to acknowledge that you made some mistakes and be open to changing your own operating style in a way that is uncomfortable for some period of time.

Because of the difficulty in facing these issues, it's sometimes wise to call on high-potential subordinates to take a fresh look at the business. This approach can be quite effective because junior employees are often not as emotionally invested as you are and can see more objectively what needs to be done. This approach is also a good way to challenge your future leaders and give them a valuable development experience. You'll give them a chance to exercise their strategic skills; you'll get a glimpse of their potential (which relates to the earlier discussion of succession planning), and you might just get some terrific new ideas for how to run the business.

This approach worked for the CEO of a high technology business in northern California, whose company had been one of the early innovators in its product space but, in recent years, had begun to falter and lose market share. In its early days, the company's primary success factors had been product innovation and satisfying customer needs. It had aggressively hired innovative engineers and marketing personnel. As new competitors emerged, customers began to focus more on cost and service (in the form of more sophisticated applications development). Stepping back, the CEO sensed that he needed to redesign the company with a different mix of people, a new organization, and a revised incentive structure. Rather than try to come up with a new model himself, he asked a more junior group of executives to formulate a new company design as if they had a "clean sheet of paper." Their study took a number of weeks, but upon completion, it led to several recommendations that the CEO immediately began to implement. For example, they suggested colocating the engineering and sales departments and creating integrated account coverage teams. They also recommended that the company push more of its engineers to interact with customers and focus on this skill in recruiting. The CEO regretted that he had not asked the question—and conducted this assignment—12 months earlier.

Even the most successful business is susceptible to new challenges posed by a changing world. Effective executives regularly look at their businesses with a clean sheet of paper—seeking advice and other perspectives from people who are less emotionally invested in the business—in order to determine whether key aspects of the way they run their organizations are still appropriate.

Leading Under Pressure

Pressure is a part of business. Changes in business conditions create urgent problems. New entrants in the market demand a competitive response. Valued employees quit, often at the most inopportune times. Leaders and their teams, no matter how smart they are, make mistakes.

The interesting thing about stressful events is that they affect each person differently—what causes you anxiety may not bother someone else, and vice versa. For some, extreme anxiety may be triggered by the prospect of a promotion; for others, by making a serious mistake; still others, by losing a piece of business to a competitor. Regardless of the source of stress, every leader experiences it, so a good question to ask yourself is: *How do I behave under pressure, and what signals am I sending my employees?*

As a leader, you're watched closely. During a crisis, your people watch you with a microscope, noting every move you make. In such times, your subordinates learn a great deal about you and what you really believe, as opposed to what you say. Do you accept responsibility for mistakes, or do you look for someone to blame? Do you support your employees, or do you turn on them? Are you cool and calm, or do you lose your temper? Do you stand up for what you believe, or do you take the expedient route and advocate what you think your seniors want to hear? You need to be self-aware enough to recognize the situations that create severe anxiety for you and manage your behavior to avoid sending unproductive messages to your people.

I've met a number of leaders who behave in a very composed and thoughtful manner the great majority of the time. Unfortunately, when they're under severe stress, they react in ways that set a very negative tone. They inadvertently train their employees to mimic that behavior and behave in a similar fashion. If your instinct is to shield yourself from blame, to take credit rather than sharing it with your subordinates, or to avoid admitting when you have made a mistake, you will give your employees license to do the same.

The CEO of a large asset-management firm was frustrated that he was unable to build a culture of accountability and teamwork in his growing business. At his request, I spoke to a number of his team members. I asked in particular about the actions of the CEO when investments they recommended declined in value. They recounted his frequent temper tantrums and accusatory diatribes, which led to an overwhelming atmosphere of blame and finger-pointing. The investment decisions had, in fact, been made jointly through a carefully constructed process involving portfolio managers, industry analysts, and the CEO. As a result of these episodes, employees learned that when investments went wrong it would be good to try to find someone else to blame. Hearing these stories, the CEO realized his actions under pressure were far more persuasive to employees than his speeches about teamwork and culture. He understood that he would have to learn to moderate his behavior under stress and, subsequently, took steps to avoid reacting so angrily to negative investment results. He also became more aware that subordinates typically felt quite regretful and demoralized when their investments declined and were more likely to need a pat on the back and coaching than a kick in the pants.

It's extremely difficult to expect employees to alert you to looming problems when they fear your reaction—and even more so when they think it's better to distance themselves from potential problems. This can create an atmosphere where surprises are, in fact, more likely as the company's natural early-warning system has been inadvertently disarmed. If you have created this kind of culture, it is quite unlikely that you will learn about problems from subordinates spontaneously—unless they want to commit career suicide.

Part of the process of maturing as a leader is learning to step back and think about what creates pressure for you, being self-aware in these situations, and disciplining your behavior to ensure that you act in a manner consistent with your core values.

Staying True to Yourself

Most business leaders ask themselves whether their leadership style fits the needs of their business. Fewer managers ask whether their style also fits their own beliefs and personality. The question here is: *Does my leadership style reflect who I truly am?*

A business career is a marathon, not a sprint, and if you aren't true to yourself, eventually you're going to wear down. As you are developing in your career, it is advisable to observe various leadership styles, and pick and choose elements that feel comfortable to you. Bear in mind, though, that observing and adopting aspects of other styles does not mean you should try to be someone else. During my career, I was fortunate to have had several superb bosses and colleagues with distinctive and unique leadership skills. While I tried to adopt some of their techniques, I also learned that I needed to develop an overall style that fit my unique skills and personality. Your style needs to fit you; even an unorthodox style can be enormously effective if it reflects your skills, values, and personality.

As you become more senior, you'll need to ask yourself an additional set of questions relating to style: *Do I assert myself sufficiently, or have I become tentative? Am I too politically correct? Does worry about my next promotion or my year-end bonus cause me to pull punches or hesitate to clearly express my views?* In many companies, ambitious executives may try to avoid confronting sensitive issues or making waves. Worse than that, they may spend an inordinate amount of energy trying to ascertain what their boss thinks and then act like they think the same thing. If they're very skilled at this, they may even get a chance to make their comments before the boss has a chance to express his opinion—and feel the warm glow of approval from the boss.

The problem is that confrontation and disagreement are crucial to effective decision making. Some of the worst decisions I've been involved in were made after a group of intelligent people had unanimously agreed to the course of action—though, later, several participants admitted that they had misgivings but were hesitant to diverge from the apparent group consensus. Conversely, it's hard for me to recall a poor decision I was involved in that was made after a thorough debate in which opposing views were vigorously expressed (even if I disagreed with the ultimate decision). Companies need their leaders to express strongly held views rather than mimic what they believe to be the party line. As a leader, therefore, you must ask yourself whether you are expressing your views or holding back and being too politic. At the same time, leaders must encourage their own subordinates to express their unvarnished opinions, make waves as appropriate, and stop tiptoeing around significant issues.

Successful leaders periodically struggle during stretches of their careers. To get back on track, they must devise techniques for stepping back, getting perspective, and developing a new game plan. In this process, having the answers is often far less important than taking time to ask yourself the right questions and gain key insights. The questions posed in this article are intended to spark your thinking. Only a subset of these may resonate with you, and you may find it more useful to come up with your own list. In either event, a self-questioning process conducted on a periodic basis will help you work through leadership challenges and issues that you invariably must tackle over the course of your career.

Originally published in January 2007. Reprint R0701H

Primal Leadership

The Hidden Driver of Great Performance. *by Daniel Goleman, Richard Boyatzis, and Annie McKee*

WHEN THE THEORY OF EMOTIONAL intelligence at work began to receive widespread attention, we frequently heard executives say—in the same breath, mind you—"That's incredible," and, "Well, I've known that all along." They were responding to our research that showed an incontrovertible link between an executive's emotional maturity, exemplified by such capabilities as self-awareness and empathy, and his or her financial performance. Simply put, the research showed that "good guys"—that is, emotionally intelligent men and women—finish first.

We've recently compiled two years of new research that, we suspect, will elicit the same kind of reaction. People will first exclaim, "No way," then quickly add, "But of course." We found that of all the elements affecting bottom-line performance, the importance of the leader's mood and its attendant behaviors are most surprising. That powerful pair set off a chain reaction: The leader's mood and behaviors drive the moods and behaviors of everyone else. A cranky and ruthless boss creates a toxic organization filled with negative underachievers who ignore opportunities; an inspirational, inclusive leader spawns acolytes for whom any challenge is surmountable. The final link in the chain is performance: profit or loss.

Our observation about the overwhelming impact of the leader's "emotional style," as we call it, is not a wholesale departure from our research into emotional intelligence. It does, however, represent a deeper analysis of our earlier assertion that a leader's emotional intelligence creates a certain culture or work environment. High levels of emotional intelligence, our research showed, create climates in which information sharing, trust, healthy risk-taking, and learning flourish. Low levels of emotional intelligence create climates rife with fear and anxiety. Because tense or terrified employees can be very productive in the short term, their organizations may post good results, but they never last.

Our investigation was designed in part to look at how emotional intelligence drives performance—in particular, at how it travels from the leader through the organization to bottom-line results. "What mechanism," we asked, "binds the chain together?" To answer that question, we turned to the latest neurological and psychological research. We also drew on our work with business leaders, observations by our colleagues of hundreds of leaders, and Hay Group data on the leadership styles of thousands of executives. From this body of research, we discovered that emotional intelligence is carried through an organization like electricity through wires. To be more specific, the leader's mood is quite literally contagious, spreading quickly and inexorably throughout the business.

We'll discuss the science of mood contagion in more depth later, but first let's turn to the key implications of our finding. If a leader's mood and accompanying behaviors are indeed such potent drivers of business success, then a leader's premier task—we would even say his primal task—is emotional leadership. A leader needs to make sure that not only is he regularly in an optimistic, authentic, high-energy mood, but also that, through his chosen actions, his followers feel and act that way, too. Managing for financial results, then, begins with the leader managing his inner life so that the right emotional and behavioral chain reaction occurs.

Managing one's inner life is not easy, of course. For many of us, it's our most difficult challenge. And accurately gauging how one's emotions affect others can be just as difficult. We know of one CEO, for example, who was certain that everyone saw him as upbeat and reliable; his direct reports told us they found his cheerfulness strained, even fake, and his decisions erratic. (We call this common

Idea in Brief

What *most* influences your company's bottom-line performance? The answer will surprise you—*and* make perfect sense: It's a leader's own mood.

Executives' emotional intelligence—their self-awareness, empathy, rapport with others—has clear links to their own performance. But new research shows that a leader's emotional style also drives everyone *else's* moods and behaviors—through a neurological process called **mood contagion**. It's akin to "Smile and the whole world smiles with you."

Emotional intelligence travels through an organization like

electricity over telephone wires. Depressed, ruthless bosses create toxic organizations filled with negative underachievers. But if you're an upbeat, inspirational leader, you cultivate positive employees who embrace and surmount even the toughest challenges.

Emotional leadership isn't just putting on a game face every day. It means understanding your impact on others—then adjusting your style accordingly. A difficult process of self-discovery—but essential *before* you can tackle your leadership responsibilities.

disconnect "CEO disease.") The implication is that primal leadership demands more than putting on a game face every day. It requires an executive to determine, through reflective analysis, how his emotional leadership drives the moods and actions of the organization, and then, with equal discipline, to adjust his behavior accordingly.

That's not to say that leaders can't have a bad day or week: Life happens. And our research doesn't suggest that good moods have to be high-pitched or nonstop—optimistic, sincere, and realistic will do. But there is no escaping the conclusion that a leader must first attend to the impact of his mood and behaviors before moving on to his wide panoply of other critical responsibilities. In this article, we introduce a process that executives can follow to assess how others experience their leadership, and we discuss ways to calibrate that impact. But first, we'll look at why moods aren't often discussed in the workplace, how the brain works to make moods contagious, and what you need to know about CEO disease.

Idea in Practice

Strengthening Your Emotional Leadership

Since few people have the guts to tell you the truth about your emotional impact, you must discover it on your own. The following process can help. It's based on brain science, as well as years of field research with executives. Use these steps to rewire your brain for greater emotional intelligence.

1. **Who do you want to be?** Imagine yourself as a highly effective leader. What do you see?

   Example: Sofia, a senior manager, often micromanaged others to ensure work was done "right." So she *imagined* herself in the future as an effective leader of her own company, enjoying trusting relationships with coworkers. She saw herself as relaxed, happy, and empowering. The exercise revealed gaps in her current emotional style.

2. **Who are you now?** To see your leadership style as others do, gather 360-degree feedback, especially from peers and subordinates. Identify your weaknesses *and* strengths.

3. **How do you get from here to there?** Devise a plan for closing the gap between who you are and who you want to be.

   Example: Juan, a marketing executive, was intimidating, impossible to please—a

No Way! Yes Way

When we said earlier that people will likely respond to our new finding by saying "No way," we weren't joking. The fact is, the emotional impact of a leader is almost never discussed in the workplace, let alone in the literature on leadership and performance. For most people, "mood" feels too personal. Even though Americans can be shockingly candid about personal matters—witness the *Jerry Springer Show* and its ilk—we are also the most legally bound. We can't even ask the age of a job applicant. Thus, a conversation about an executive's mood or the moods he creates in his employees might be construed as an invasion of privacy.

We also might avoid talking about a leader's emotional style and its impact because, frankly, the topic feels soft. When was the last time you evaluated a subordinate's mood as part of her performance grouch. Charged with growing his company, he *needed* to be encouraging, optimistic—a coach with a vision. Setting out to understand others, he coached soccer, volunteered at a crisis center, and got to know subordinates by meeting outside of work. These new situations stimulated him to break old habits and try new responses.

4. **How do you make change stick?** Repeatedly rehearse new behaviors—physically *and* mentally—until they're automatic.

   Example: Tom, an executive, wanted to learn how to coach rather than castigate struggling employees. Using his commuting time to visualize a difficult meeting with one employee, he envisioned asking questions and listening, and mentally rehearsed how he'd handle feeling impatient. This exercise prepared him to adopt new behaviors at the actual meeting.

5. **Who can help you?** Don't try to build your emotional skills alone—identify others who can help you navigate this difficult process. Managers at Unilever formed learning groups that helped them strengthen their leadership abilities by exchanging frank feedback and developing strong mutual trust.

appraisal? You may have alluded to it—"Your work is hindered by an often negative perspective," or "Your enthusiasm is terrific"—but it is unlikely you mentioned mood outright, let alone discussed its impact on the organization's results.

And yet our research undoubtedly will elicit a "But of course" reaction, too. Everyone knows how much a leader's emotional state drives performance because everyone has had, at one time or another, the inspirational experience of working for an upbeat manager or the crushing experience of toiling for a sour-spirited boss. The former made everything feel possible, and as a result, stretch goals were achieved, competitors beaten, and new customers won. The latter made work grueling. In the shadow of the boss's dark mood, other parts of the organization became "the enemy," colleagues became suspicious of one another, and customers slipped away.

Our research, and research by other social scientists, confirms the verity of these experiences. (There are, of course, rare cases when a brutal boss produces terrific results. We explore that dynamic in the sidebar "Those Wicked Bosses Who Win.") The studies are too numerous to mention here but, in aggregate, they show that when the leader is in a happy mood, the people around him view everything in a more positive light. That, in turn, makes them optimistic about achieving their goals, enhances their creativity and the efficiency of their decision making, and predisposes them to be helpful. Research conducted by Alice Isen at Cornell in 1999, for example, found that an upbeat environment fosters mental efficiency, making people better at taking in and understanding information, at using decision rules in complex judgments, and at being flexible in their thinking. Other research directly links mood and financial performance. In 1986, for instance, Martin Seligman and Peter Schulman of the University of Pennsylvania demonstrated that insurance agents who had a "glass half-full" outlook were far more able than their more pessimistic peers to persist despite rejections, and thus, they closed more sales. (For more information on these studies and a list of our research base, visit www.eiconsortium.org.)

Many leaders whose emotional styles create a dysfunctional environment are eventually fired. (Of course, that's rarely the stated reason; poor results are.) But it doesn't have to end that way. Just as a bad mood can be turned around, so can the spread of toxic feelings from an emotionally inept leader. A look inside the brain explains both why and how.

The Science of Moods

A growing body of research on the human brain proves that, for better or worse, leaders' moods affect the emotions of the people around them. The reason for that lies in what scientists call the open-loop nature of the brain's limbic system, our emotional center. A closed-loop system is self-regulating, whereas an open-loop system depends on external sources to manage itself. In other words, we rely on connections with other people to determine our moods. The

Those Wicked Bosses Who Win

Everyone knows of a rude and coercive CEO who, by all appearances, epitomizes the antithesis of emotional intelligence yet seems to reap great business results. If a leader's mood matters so much, how can we explain those mean-spirited, successful SOBs?

First, let's take a closer look at them. Just because a particular executive is the most visible, he may not actually lead the company. A CEO who heads a conglomerate may have no followers to speak of; it's his division heads who actively lead people and affect profitability.

Second, sometimes an SOB leader has strengths that counterbalance his caustic behavior, but they don't attract as much attention in the business press. In his early days at GE, Jack Welch exhibited a strong hand at the helm as he undertook a radical company turnaround. At that time and in that situation, Welch's firm, top-down style was appropriate. What got less press was how Welch subsequently settled into a more emotionally intelligent leadership style, especially when he articulated a new vision for the company and mobilized people to follow it.

Those caveats aside, let's get back to those infamous corporate leaders who seem to have achieved sterling business results despite their brutish approaches to leadership. Skeptics cite Bill Gates, for example, as a leader who gets away with a harsh style that should theoretically damage his company.

But our leadership model, which shows the effectiveness of specific leadership styles in specific situations, puts Gates's supposedly negative behaviors in a different light. (Our model is explained in detail in the HBR article "Leadership That Gets Results," which appeared in the March–April 2000 issue.) Gates is the achievement-driven leader par excellence, in an organization that has cherry-picked highly talented and motivated people. His apparently harsh leadership style—baldly challenging employees to surpass their past performance—can be quite effective when employees are competent, motivated, and need little direction—all characteristics of Microsoft's engineers.

In short, it's all too easy for a skeptic to argue against the importance of leaders who manage their moods by citing a "rough and tough" leader who achieved good business results despite his bad behavior. We contend that there are, of course, exceptions to the rule, and that in some specific business cases, an SOB boss resonates just fine. But in general, leaders who are jerks must reform or else their moods and actions will eventually catch up with them.

open-loop limbic system was a winning design in evolution because it let people come to one another's emotional rescue—enabling a mother, for example, to soothe her crying infant.

The open-loop design serves the same purpose today as it did thousands of years ago. Research in intensive care units has shown, for example, that the comforting presence of another person not only lowers the patient's blood pressure but also slows the secretion of fatty acids that block arteries. Another study found that three or more incidents of intense stress within a year (for example, serious financial trouble, being fired, or a divorce) triples the death rate in socially isolated middle-aged men, but it has no impact on the death rate of men with many close relationships.

Scientists describe the open loop as "interpersonal limbic regulation"; one person transmits signals that can alter hormone levels, cardiovascular functions, sleep rhythms, even immune functions, inside the body of another. That's how couples are able to trigger surges of oxytocin in each other's brains, creating a pleasant, affectionate feeling. But in all aspects of social life, our physiologies intermingle. Our limbic system's open-loop design lets other people change our very physiology and hence, our emotions.

Even though the open loop is so much a part of our lives, we usually don't notice the process. Scientists have captured the attunement of emotions in the laboratory by measuring the physiology—such as heart rate—of two people sharing a good conversation. As the interaction begins, their bodies operate at different rhythms. But after 15 minutes, the physiological profiles of their bodies look remarkably similar.

Researchers have seen again and again how emotions spread irresistibly in this way whenever people are near one another. As far back as 1981, psychologists Howard Friedman and Ronald Riggio found that even completely nonverbal expressiveness can affect other people. For example, when three strangers sit facing one another in silence for a minute or two, the most emotionally expressive of the three transmits his or her mood to the other two—without a single word being spoken.

Smile and the World Smiles with You

Remember that old cliché? It's not too far from the truth. As we've shown, mood contagion is a real neurological phenomenon, but not all emotions spread with the same ease. A 1999 study conducted by Sigal Barsade at the Yale School of Management showed that, among working groups, cheerfulness and warmth spread easily, while irritability caught on less so, and depression least of all.

It should come as no surprise that laughter is the most contagious of all emotions. Hearing laughter, we find it almost impossible not to laugh or smile, too. That's because some of our brain's open-loop circuits are designed to detect smiles and laughter, making us respond in kind. Scientists theorize that this dynamic was hardwired into our brains ages ago because smiles and laughter had a way of cementing alliances, thus helping the species survive.

The main implication here for leaders undertaking the primal task of managing their moods and the moods of others is this: Humor hastens the spread of an upbeat climate. But like the leader's mood in general, humor must resonate with the organization's culture and its reality. Smiles and laughter, we would posit, are only contagious when they're genuine.

The same holds true in the office, boardroom, or shop floor; group members inevitably "catch" feelings from one another. In 2000, Caroline Bartel at New York University and Richard Saavedra at the University of Michigan found that in 70 work teams across diverse industries, people in meetings together ended up sharing moods—both good and bad—within two hours. One study asked teams of nurses and accountants to monitor their moods over weeks; researchers discovered that their emotions tracked together, and they were largely independent of each team's shared hassles. Groups, therefore, like individuals, ride emotional roller coasters, sharing everything from jealousy to angst to euphoria. (A good mood, incidentally, spreads most swiftly by the judicious use of humor. For more on this, see the sidebar "Smile and the World Smiles with You.")

Moods that start at the top tend to move the fastest because everyone watches the boss. They take their emotional cues from him. Even when the boss isn't highly visible—for example, the CEO

Get Happy, Carefully

Good moods galvanize good performance, but it doesn't make sense for a leader to be as chipper as a blue jay at dawn if sales are tanking or the business is going under. The most effective executives display moods and behaviors that match the situation at hand, with a healthy dose of optimism mixed in. They respect how other people are feeling—even if it is glum or defeated—but they also model what it looks like to move forward with hope and humor.

This kind of performance, which we call resonance, is for all intents and purposes the four components of emotional intelligence in action.

Self-awareness, perhaps the most essential of the emotional intelligence competencies, is the ability to read your own emotions. It allows people to know their strengths and limitations and feel confident about their self-worth. Resonant leaders use self-awareness to gauge their own moods accurately, and they intuitively know how they are affecting others.

Self-management is the ability to control your emotions and act with honesty and integrity in reliable and adaptable ways. Resonant leaders don't let their occasional bad moods seize the day; they use self-management to leave it outside the office or to explain its source to people in a reasonable manner, so they know where it's coming from and how long it might last.

Social awareness includes the key capabilities of empathy and organizational intuition. Socially aware executives do more than sense other people's emotions, they show that they care. Further, they are experts at reading the currents of office politics. Thus, resonant leaders often keenly understand how their words and actions make others feel, and they are sensitive enough to change them when that impact is negative.

Relationship management, the last of the emotional intelligence competencies, includes the abilities to communicate clearly and convincingly, disarm

---

who works behind closed doors on an upper floor—his attitude affects the moods of his direct reports, and a domino effect ripples throughout the company.

Call That CEO a Doctor

If the leader's mood is so important, then he or she had better get into a good one, right? Yes, but the full answer is more complicated than that. A leader's mood has the greatest impact on performance

conflicts, and build strong personal bonds. Resonant leaders use these skills to spread their enthusiasm and solve disagreements, often with humor and kindness.

As effective as resonant leadership is, it is just as rare. Most people suffer through dissonant leaders whose toxic moods and upsetting behaviors wreak havoc before a hopeful and realistic leader repairs the situation.

Consider what happened recently at an experimental division of the BBC, the British media giant. Even though the group's 200 or so journalists and editors had given their best effort, management decided to close the division.

The shutdown itself was bad enough, but the brusque, contentious mood and manner of the executive sent to deliver the news to the assembled staff incited something beyond the expected frustration. People became enraged—at both the decision and the bearer of the news. The executive's cranky mood and delivery created an atmosphere so threatening that he had to call security to be ushered from the room.

The next day, another executive visited the same staff. His mood was somber and respectful, as was his behavior. He spoke about the importance of journalism to the vibrancy of a society and of the calling that had drawn them all to the field in the first place. He reminded them that no one goes into journalism to get rich—as a profession its finances have always been marginal, job security ebbing and flowing with the larger economic tides. He recalled a time in his own career when he had been let go and how he had struggled to find a new position—but how he had stayed dedicated to the profession. Finally, he wished them well in getting on with their careers.

The reaction from what had been an angry mob the day before? When this resonant leader finished speaking, the staff cheered.

---

when it is upbeat. But it must also be in tune with those around him. We call this dynamic *resonance*. (For more on this, see the sidebar "Get Happy, Carefully.")

We found that an alarming number of leaders do not really know if they have resonance with their organizations. Rather, they suffer from CEO disease; its one unpleasant symptom is the sufferer's near-total ignorance about how his mood and actions appear to the organization. It's not that leaders don't care how they are perceived; most do. But they incorrectly assume that they can decipher this information themselves. Worse, they think that if they are having a negative effect, someone will tell them. They're wrong.

As one CEO in our research explains, "I so often feel I'm not getting the truth. I can never put my finger on it, because no one is actually lying to me. But I can sense that people are hiding information or camouflaging key facts. They aren't lying, but neither are they telling me everything I need to know. I'm always second-guessing."

People don't tell leaders the whole truth about their emotional impact for many reasons. Sometimes they are scared of being the bearer of bad news—and getting shot. Others feel it isn't their place to comment on such a personal topic. Still others don't realize that what they really want to talk about is the effects of the leader's emotional style—that feels too vague. Whatever the reason, the CEO can't rely on his followers to spontaneously give him the full picture.

Taking Stock

The process we recommend for self-discovery and personal reinvention is neither newfangled nor born of pop psychology, like so many self-help programs offered to executives today. Rather, it is based on three streams of research into how executives can improve the emotional intelligence capabilities most closely linked to effective leadership. (Information on these research streams can also be found at www.eiconsortium.org.). In 1989, one of us (Richard Boyatzis) began drawing on this body of research to design the five-step process itself, and since then, thousands of executives have used it successfully.

Unlike more traditional forms of coaching, our process is based on brain science. A person's emotional skills—the attitude and abilities with which someone approaches life and work—are not genetically hardwired, like eye color and skin tone. But in some ways they might as well be, because they are so deeply embedded in our neurology.

A person's emotional skills do, in fact, have a genetic component. Scientists have discovered, for instance, the gene for shyness—which is not a mood, per se, but it can certainly drive a person toward a persistently quiet demeanor, which may be read as a "down" mood. Other people are preternaturally jolly—that is, their relentless cheerfulness seems preternatural until you meet their peppy parents. As one executive explains, "All I know is that ever since I was a baby, I have always been happy. It drives some people crazy, but I couldn't get blue if I tried. And my brother is the exact same way; he saw the bright side of life, even during his divorce."

Even though emotional skills are partly inborn, experience plays a major role in how the genes are expressed. A happy baby whose parents die or who endures physical abuse may grow into a melancholy adult. A cranky toddler may turn into a cheerful adult after discovering a fulfilling avocation. Still, research suggests that our range of emotional skills is relatively set by our mid-20s and that our accompanying behaviors are, by that time, deep-seated habits. And therein lies the rub: The more we act a certain way—be it happy, depressed, or cranky—the more the behavior becomes ingrained in our brain circuitry, and the more we will continue to feel and act that way.

That's why emotional intelligence matters so much for a leader. An emotionally intelligent leader can monitor his or her moods through self-awareness, change them for the better through self-management, understand their impact through empathy, and act in ways that boost others' moods through relationship management.

The following five-part process is designed to rewire the brain toward more emotionally intelligent behaviors. The process begins with imagining your ideal self and then coming to terms with your real self, as others experience you. The next step is creating a tactical plan to bridge the gap between ideal and real, and after that, to practice those activities. It concludes with creating a community of colleagues and family—call them change enforcers—to keep the process alive. Let's look at the steps in more detail.

"Who do I want to be?"

Sofia, a senior manager at a northern European telecommunications company, knew she needed to understand how her emotional leadership affected others. Whenever she felt stressed, she tended to communicate poorly and take over subordinates' work so that the job would be done "right." Attending leadership seminars hadn't changed her habits, and neither had reading management books or working with mentors.

When Sofia came to us, we asked her to imagine herself eight years from now as an effective leader and to write a description of a typical day. "What would she be doing?" we asked. "Where would she live? Who would be there? How would it feel?" We urged her to consider her deepest values and loftiest dreams and to explain how those ideals had become a part of her everyday life.

Sofia pictured herself leading her own tight-knit company staffed by ten colleagues. She was enjoying an open relationship with her daughter and had trusting relationships with her friends and coworkers. She saw herself as a relaxed and happy leader and parent, and as loving and empowering to all those around her.

In general, Sofia had a low level of self-awareness: She was rarely able to pinpoint why she was struggling at work and at home. All she could say was, "Nothing is working right." This exercise, which prompted her to picture what life would look like if everything were going right, opened her eyes to the missing elements in her emotional style. She was able to see the impact she had on people in her life.

"Who am I now?"

In the next step of the discovery process, you come to see your leadership style as others do. This is both difficult and dangerous. Difficult, because few people have the guts to tell the boss or a colleague what he's really like. And dangerous, because such information can sting or even paralyze. A small bit of ignorance about yourself isn't always a bad thing: Ego-defense mechanisms have their advantages. Research by Martin Seligman shows that high-functioning people generally feel more optimistic about their prospects and possibilities than average performers. Their rose-colored lenses, in fact, fuel the enthusiasm and energy that make the unexpected and the extraordinary achievable. Playwright Henrik Ibsen called such self-delusions "vital lies," soothing mistruths we let ourselves believe in order to face a daunting world.

But self-delusion should come in very small doses. Executives should relentlessly seek the truth about themselves, especially since it is sure to be somewhat diluted when they hear it anyway. One way to get the truth is to keep an extremely open attitude toward critiques. Another is to seek out negative feedback, even cultivating a colleague or two to play devil's advocate.

We also highly recommend gathering feedback from as many people as possible—including bosses, peers, and subordinates. Feedback from subordinates and peers is especially helpful because it most accurately predicts a leader's effectiveness, two, four, and even seven years out, according to research by Glenn McEvoy at Utah State and Richard Beatty at Rutgers University.

Of course, 360-degree feedback doesn't specifically ask people to evaluate your moods, actions, and their impact. But it does reveal how people experience you. For instance, when people rate how well you listen, they are really reporting how well they think you hear them. Similarly, when 360-degree feedback elicits ratings about coaching effectiveness, the answers show whether or not people feel you understand and care about them. When the feedback uncovers low scores on, say, openness to new ideas, it means that people experience you as inaccessible or unapproachable or both. In sum, all you need to know about your emotional impact is in 360-degree feedback, if you look for it.

One last note on this second step. It is, of course, crucial to identify your areas of weakness. But focusing only on your weaknesses can be dispiriting. That's why it is just as important, maybe even more so, to understand your strengths. Knowing where your real self overlaps with your ideal self will give you the positive energy you need to move forward to the next step in the process—bridging the gaps.

"How do I get from here to there?"
Once you know who you want to be and have compared it with how people see you, you need to devise an action plan. For Sofia, this meant planning for a real improvement in her level of self-awareness. So she asked each member of her team at work to give her feedback—weekly, anonymously, and in written form—about her mood

and performance and their affect on people. She also committed herself to three tough but achievable tasks: spending an hour each day reflecting on her behavior in a journal, taking a class on group dynamics at a local college, and enlisting the help of a trusted colleague as an informal coach.

Consider, too, how Juan, a marketing executive for the Latin American division of a major integrated energy company, completed this step. Juan was charged with growing the company in his home country of Venezuela as well as in the entire region—a job that would require him to be a coach and a visionary and to have an encouraging, optimistic outlook. Yet 360-degree feedback revealed that Juan was seen as intimidating and internally focused. Many of his direct reports saw him as a grouch—impossible to please at his worst, and emotionally draining at his best.

Identifying this gap allowed Juan to craft a plan with manageable steps toward improvement. He knew he needed to hone his powers of empathy if he wanted to develop a coaching style, so he committed to various activities that would let him practice that skill. For instance, Juan decided to get to know each of his subordinates better; if he understood more about who they were, he thought, he'd be more able to help them reach their goals. He made plans with each employee to meet outside of work, where they might be more comfortable revealing their feelings.

Juan also looked for areas outside of his job to forge his missing links—for example, coaching his daughter's soccer team and volunteering at a local crisis center. Both activities helped him to experiment with how well he understood others and to try out new behaviors.

Again, let's look at the brain science at work. Juan was trying to overcome ingrained behaviors—his approach to work had taken hold over time, without his realizing it. Bringing them into awareness was a crucial step toward changing them. As he paid more attention, the situations that arose—while listening to a colleague, coaching soccer, or talking on the phone to someone who was distraught—all became cues that stimulated him to break old habits and try new responses.

Resonance in Times of Crisis

When talking about leaders' moods, the importance of resonance cannot be overstated. While our research suggests that leaders should generally be up-beat, their behavior must be rooted in realism, especially when faced with a crisis.

Consider the response of Bob Mulholland, senior VP and head of the client relations group at Merrill Lynch, to the terrorist attacks in New York. On September 11, 2001, Mulholland and his staff in Two World Financial Center felt the building rock, then watched as smoke poured out of a gaping hole in the building directly across from theirs. People started panicking: Some ran frantically from window to window. Others were paralyzed with fear. Those with relatives working in the World Trade Center were terrified for their safety. Mulholland knew he had to act: "When there's a crisis, you've got to show people the way, step by step, and make sure you're taking care of their concerns."

He started by getting people the information they needed to "unfreeze." He found out, for instance, which floors employees' relatives worked on and assured them that they'd have enough time to escape. Then he calmed the panic-stricken, one at a time. "We're getting out of here now," he said quietly, "and you're coming with me. Not the elevator, take the stairs." He remained calm and decisive, yet he didn't minimize people's emotional responses. Thanks to him, everyone escaped before the towers collapsed.

Mulholland's leadership didn't end there. Recognizing that this event would touch each client personally, he and his team devised a way for financial consultants to connect with their clients on an emotional level. They called every client to ask, "How are you? Are your loved ones okay? How are you feeling?" As Mulholland explains, "There was no way to pick up and do business as usual. The first order of 'business' was letting our clients know we really do care."

Bob Mulholland courageously performed one of the most crucial emotional tasks of leadership: He helped himself and his people find meaning in the face of chaos and madness. To do so, he first attuned to and expressed the shared emotional reality. That's why the direction he eventually articulated resonated at the gut level. His words and his actions reflected what people were feeling in their hearts.

This cueing for habit change is neural as well as perceptual. Researchers at the University of Pittsburgh and Carnegie Mellon University have shown that as we mentally prepare for a task, we activate the prefrontal cortex—the part of the brain that moves us into action. The greater the prior activation, the better we do at the task.

Such mental preparation becomes particularly important when we're trying to replace an old habit with a better one. As neuroscientist Cameron Carter at the University of Pittsburgh found, the prefrontal cortex becomes particularly active when a person prepares to overcome a habitual response. The aroused prefrontal cortex marks the brain's focus on what's about to happen. Without that arousal, a person will reenact tried-and-true but undesirable routines: The executive who just doesn't listen will once again cut off his subordinate, a ruthless leader will launch into yet another critical attack, and so on. That's why a learning agenda is so important. Without one, we literally do not have the brainpower to change.

"How do I make change stick?"
In short, making change last requires practice. The reason, again, lies in the brain. It takes doing and redoing, over and over, to break old neural habits. A leader must rehearse a new behavior until it becomes automatic—that is, until he's mastered it at the level of implicit learning. Only then will the new wiring replace the old.

While it is best to practice new behaviors, as Juan did, sometimes just envisioning them will do. Take the case of Tom, an executive who wanted to close the gap between his real self (perceived by colleagues and subordinates to be cold and hard driving) and his ideal self (a visionary and a coach).

Tom's learning plan involved finding opportunities to step back and coach his employees rather than jumping down their throats when he sensed they were wrong. Tom also began to spend idle moments during his commute thinking through how to handle encounters he would have that day. One morning, while en route to a breakfast meeting with an employee who seemed to be bungling a project, Tom ran through a positive scenario in his mind. He asked questions and listened to be sure he fully understood the situation before trying to solve the problem. He anticipated feeling impatient, and he rehearsed how he would handle these feelings.

Studies on the brain affirm the benefits of Tom's visualization technique: Imagining something in vivid detail can fire the same brain cells actually involved in doing that activity. The new brain circuitry appears to go through its paces, strengthening connections, even when we merely repeat the sequence in our minds. So to alleviate the fears associated with trying out riskier ways of leading, we should first visualize some likely scenarios. Doing so will make us feel less awkward when we actually put the new skills into practice.

Experimenting with new behaviors and seizing opportunities inside and outside of work to practice them—as well as using such methods as mental rehearsal—eventually triggers in our brains the neural connections necessary for genuine change to occur. Even so, lasting change doesn't happen through experimentation and brainpower alone. We need, as the song goes, a little help from our friends.

"Who can help me?"

The fifth step in the self-discovery and reinvention process is creating a community of supporters. Take, for example, managers at Unilever who formed learning groups as part of their executive development process. At first, they gathered to discuss their careers and how to provide leadership. But because they were also charged with discussing their dreams and their learning goals, they soon realized that they were discussing both their work and their personal lives. They developed a strong mutual trust and began relying on one another for frank feedback as they worked on strengthening their leadership abilities. When this happens, the business benefits through stronger performance. Many professionals today have created similar groups, and for good reason. People we trust let us try out unfamiliar parts of our leadership repertoire without risk.

We cannot improve our emotional intelligence or change our leadership style without help from others. We not only practice with other people but also rely on them to create a safe environment in which to experiment. We need to get feedback about how our actions affect others and to assess our progress on our learning agenda.

In fact, perhaps paradoxically, in the self-directed learning process we draw on others every step of the way—from articulating and refining our ideal self and comparing it with the reality to the final assessment that affirms our progress. Our relationships offer us the very context in which we understand our progress and comprehend the usefulness of what we're learning.

Mood over Matter

When we say that managing your mood and the moods of your followers is the task of primal leadership, we certainly don't mean to suggest that mood is all that matters. As we've noted, your actions are critical, and mood and actions together must resonate with the organization and with reality. Similarly, we acknowledge all the other challenges leaders must conquer—from strategy to hiring to new product development. It's all in a long day's work.

But taken as a whole, the message sent by neurological, psychological, and organizational research is startling in its clarity. Emotional leadership is the spark that ignites a company's performance, creating a bonfire of success or a landscape of ashes. Moods matter that much.

Originally published in December 2001. Reprint R0111C

About the Contributors

RICHARD BOYATZIS chairs the department of organizational behavior at the Weatherhead School of Management at Case Western Reserve University.

HEIKE BRUCH is a professor of leadership at the University of St. Gallen in Switzerland.

CLAYTON M. CHRISTENSEN is the Robert and Jane Cizik Professor of Business Administration at Harvard Business School.

DIANE L. COUTU is a former senior editor of *Harvard Business Review*.

STEPHEN R. COVEY is vice chairman of Franklin Covey, a global provider of leadership development and productivity services.

PETER F. DRUCKER was a professor of social science and management at Claremont Graduate University in California.

STEWART D. FRIEDMAN is the Practice Professor of Management at the University of Pennsylvania's Wharton School.

SUMANTRA GHOSHAL was a professor of strategy and international management at London Business School.

DANIEL GOLEMAN cochairs the Consortium for Research on Emotional Intelligence in Organizations at Rutgers University.

EDWARD M. HALLOWELL is a psychiatrist and the founder of the Hallowell Centers for Cognitive and Emotional Health.

ROBERT S. KAPLAN is a professor of management practice at Harvard Business School.

CATHERINE McCARTHY is a senior vice president at the Energy Project in New York.

ANNIE McKEE is on the faculty of the University of Pennsylvania's Graduate School of Education.

WILLIAM ONCKEN, JR., was chairman of the William Oncken Corporation, a management consulting company.

ROBERT E. QUINN is the Margaret Elliott Tracy Collegiate Professor in Business Administration at the University of Michigan's Ross School of Business.

TONY SCHWARTZ is the president and founder of the Energy Project in New York.

DONALD L. WASS heads the Dallas–Fort Worth region of The Executive Committee (TEC), an international organization for presidents and CEOs.

Index

accountability, 164–165
action, bias for, 126
adaptation, 108–109
Adaptiv Learning Systems, 49
ADT. *See* attention deficit trait (ADT)
alignment, 76, 116–117, 155, 162–163
Andersson, Dan, 119, 124–126
Andrews, Mike, 58
Anspacher, Jonathan, 74
appreciation, expressing, 64, 71
arrogance, 14–15
assessment. *See* self-assessment
assumptions, questioning, 107
attention deficit disorder (ADD), 80, 81, 83–84
attention deficit trait (ADT), 79–95
  ADD compared with, 81, 83–84
  managing, 80, 87–93
  organizational culture and, 82, 87, 88–89, 93–95
  symptoms of, 79
audits, energy, 67, 68–69
authenticity, 100, 170–171

Babin, Nicolas, 72
balance, 33, 34, 38–39, 97–114.
  See also discretionary time
Barsade, Sigal, 177
Bartel, Caroline, 177
BBC, 179
Beatty, Richard, 183
Becker, Dean, 49
Beethoven, Ludwig von, 19–20
Bessemer Venture Partners, 7
"Beware the Busy Manager" (Ghoshal and Bruch), 115
boss-imposed time, 33, 45
brain
  ADD and, 81, 83
  ADT and, 82, 84–87, 88–89
  emotional intelligence and, 172, 174, 176, 181–188

brain-derived neurotrophic factor (BDNF), 90
breaks, taking, 63, 64, 67, 69, 78
breathing, abdominal, 64, 70–72, 78
bricolage, 57–60
Buford, Bob, 30
business school students
  purpose in life and career decisions of, 4–5
  rewards of a career in business for, 4
"buying time" ritual, 70–72

Calvin, John, 14
Cantor Fitzgerald, 53
career management, 3–5, 14–17, 20–21, 24–25, 29–32
Carter, Cameron, 186
Catholic Church, 56
CEO disease, 171–172, 179–180
change, 15–16, 126
  maintaining, 173, 181, 184, 186–187
  signs of needed, 15–16, 141–142
  steps in, 112–113
Chen, Kenneth, 98, 102–103, 109
Chun, Patrick, 6
Churchill, Winston, 19
Cluna, Dan, 72–73
coaching and mentoring, 15–16, 20, 101–102
  peer, 101–102
  resilience, 55–56
  self-assessment of, 154, 157–160
Coleman, John, 7
Collins, Jim, 52, 57
comfort seeking, 128–129
communication
  emotional leadership and, 178–179
  face-to-face, 44, 89
  self-assessment of, 166

initiative in, 35, 36
motives in, 36
in practice, 36
status updates in, 36
transferring initiative for,
42–43
trust and, 36
who is working for whom in,
37–39
moods, contagiousness of, 169–188
morale, 158
Morgan Stanley, 53–54, 60
motivation, 36, 62
Mulholland, Bob, 185
multitasking, 72

Neeleman, David, 83–84, 94–95
nerve growth factor (NGF), 90
Nishida, Fujio, 70–71, 77

OHIO (only handle it once) rule,
82, 91
Oiseaux, Jackie, 54–55
openness, external, 129, 130,
131–132, 141–142
opportunities, 15, 24–25, 115–116
optimism, 52–53, 178–179
organization, 79–80, 81–82, 90–91,
106, 162–163
organizational culture
ADT and, 82, 87, 88–89,
93–95
of empowerment, 40, 116–117
energy management and, 65,
77–78
humor and, 177
leadership under pressure and,
163–165
resilience and, 56–57, 59–60
trust in, 28–29
values and, 22–23
overload, 55, 70, 79–95, 92

The Path of Least Resistance (Fritz),
128–129
Patton, George, 20
performance
emotional styles and, 169–188
energy management and, 62–66
feedback analysis and, 14
fundamental leadership and,
144–145
time of day and, 91
Total Leadership and, 99
work styles and, 16, 17–21
performance reviews, 158, 172–173.
See also feedback
perseverance, 74, 83
personalities, 17–21, 151, 155,
165–166
personality, 27–28
personal strategy
career decisions of students and,
4–5, 6
creating, 4–6
humility and, 11–12
marginal costs concept and life of
integrity in, 3, 10–11
metric for measuring, 12
motivators for career decisions
and, 3
purpose in life and, 4–5
resource allocation decisions and,
3, 4, 6–8
perspective, 50, 64, 71–72
Phillip Morris, 57
planning, 82, 106
career, 26
resilience and, 53–54
for second careers, 30–31
succession, 151, 154–155, 160–161
Prahalad, C.K., 142
primal leadership, 169–188
priorities, 38, 107, 118
ADT and, 79–80, 82, 91

The most important management ideas all in one place.

We hope you enjoyed this book from *Harvard Business Review*. Now you can get even more with HBR's 10 Must Reads Boxed Set. From books on leadership and strategy to managing yourself and others, this 6-book collection delivers articles on the most essential business topics to help you succeed.

HBR's 10 Must Reads Series

The definitive collection of ideas and best practices on our most sought-after topics from the best minds in business.

- Change Management
- Collaboration
- Communication
- Emotional Intelligence
- Innovation
- Leadership
- Making Smart Decisions

- Managing Across Cultures
- Managing People
- Managing Yourself
- Strategic Marketing
- Strategy
- Teams
- The Essentials

hbr.org/mustreads

Buy for your team, clients, or event.
Visit hbr.org/bulksales for quantity discount rates.

Harvard
Business
Review
Press